Generation RISK

Generation RISK

How to Protect Your Teenager from Smoking and Other Dangerous Behavior

CORKY NEWTON

M. Evans and Company, Inc.
New York

M. Evans and Company, Inc.
216 East 49th Street
New York, New York 10017

Library of Congress Cataloging-in-Publication Data

Newton, Corky.
    Generation risk : how to protect your teen from smoking and other dangerous behavior / by Corky Newton.
      p. cm.
    ISBN 0-87131-940-3
    1. Teenagers—Tobacco use—Prevention. 2. Risk-taking (Psychology) in adolescence—United States. 3. Parent and teenager—United States. 4. Parenting—United States. I. Title
HV5745 .N49 2001
649'.125—dc21

                                      00-060000

Printed in the United States of America

9 8 7 6 5 4 3 2 1

To my Dad, the world's best role model.

He gave me this advice when I was a teenager leaving home for college:

"Remember all the things I told you to do, and all the things I told you not to do, and for heaven's sake, try not to get the two mixed up!"

CONTENTS

FOREWORD

TEENAGERS ARE PRESENTED with alarming degrees of freedom and exposure in this electronic age of fast living and high risk, at possibly the most critical time of their lives. What is unique about this generation is their attitude toward risk, which makes them more daring and, at the same time, more vulnerable than any generation before. Kids today thrive on risk and often ignore its consequences, challenging parents to find ways to combat the dangers that abound during the teenage years.

As president of the nation's first health education center, I can attest to the fact that parents need help in addressing critical issues with their teenage children. The threats of smoking, drinking, drug abuse, and early sexual activity weigh heavily on all parents, but most are at a loss about how to approach these topics knowledgeably and in a way that will have a positive impact on their children's behavior.

Generation Risk is a powerful breakthrough book in parent-teen relationships. It teaches us how to relate to today's teenagers and how to protect them from the dangerous risks they seem to seek out.

As head of Brown & Williamson Tobacco Corporation's youth smoking prevention program, Corky Newton knows about risks, about tobacco, and about kids. She has put together an amazing collection of penetrating insights and bold ideas tempered by sensitivity and warmth to offer parents guidance in dealing with the teenagers of this new generation.

As a health educator and youth advocate, I wholeheartedly endorse this book for a number of reasons.

First, the book represents a landmark in analyzing the unique characteristics of the new generation the author has so correctly labeled *Generation Risk*. For parents, it provides a startlingly clear picture of this generation, its motivations, and its culture. Without the insights presented in this book, many parents would be hard-pressed to fully understand the children of this generation—never mind persuading them to make healthier choices.

Second, this book offers concrete ideas that parents can employ for more effective communication about these issues with their teens. Parents learn why the word "don't" can backfire with teens. They find out how to handle the issue if they, the parents, are smokers themselves. They discover what steps they can take if, despite their best efforts, they find their teen has started smoking.

Third, this book comes from an unlikely but extremely knowledgeable source. Who knows tobacco and its effects better than a tobacco executive? I believe that in assisting parents in this area, the author signals that a new era has begun for tobacco companies, one in which they recognize the responsibility they hold in preventing teens from taking up smoking in the first place.

For more than a quarter-century, we at the Robert Crown Center for Health Education in Hinsdale, Illinois, a suburb of Chicago, have been educating young people about making healthy choices for their bodies. Nearly four million students have attended our programs on general health, drug abuse prevention, and sex education topics. Our programs present strong antismoking messages complete with engaging exhibits and high-impact audio-visuals.

However, in the past decade research shows that while our programs can have a lifelong and memorable impact, they alone are not enough. Researchers are telling us that parents are the most important factor in fighting the war against dangerous risk-taking by teenagers.

As health educators, we know that we cannot do it alone. Programs like D.A.R.E. to help kids resist drugs and violence are not enough, and neither are oversimplified "Just Say No" ad campaigns. All forces—from schools to social agencies to the media—must work together to address the problem.

But parents are the ones who are going to make the difference when it comes to actually changing behavior.

Just when parents are increasingly realizing they must play an active role in preventing dangerous behavior like smoking in their teenage children, Corky Newton has written a revolutionary book that can make a difference in the future of our children. Our young people deserve the brightest, healthiest, and most successful tomorrows possible, and as a parent you owe it to yourself and to your teenager to read this book.

—*John P. Zaremba, Ph.D.*
President of the Robert Crown Center
for Health Education

PREFACE

IF YOU DON'T WANT your teenager to smoke, *this is the book you should read.* As vice president of a multibillion-dollar tobacco corporation, I can arm you with a powerful weapon to keep your teenager from smoking: information about cigarettes and smoking *from inside a tobacco company.*

As Vice President of Corporate Responsibility and Youth Smoking Prevention for Brown & Williamson Tobacco Corporation, a major company within British American Tobacco, I understand why kids smoke and take other risks, and I can help parents *prevent their teenagers from smoking.*

In fact, parents facing teenagers today are dealing with a whole new set of problems. In the context of other risks, many teens consider smoking cigarettes to be harmless. Teenagers today have access to information, mobility, freedom, and an attitude of entitlement that earns their generation a bold new name: *Generation Risk.*

The risks these teenagers embrace are complicated and interrelated, and parents need new approaches and better information to cope with them. For all their bravado, this generation of teenagers is still highly vulnerable, but they are difficult to reach. If parents want to have an impact on Generation Risk, they can't rely on conventional wisdom and traditional techniques. Educational programs of the past have been extraordinarily unsuccessful in preventing smoking and drug use among the latest generation of teenagers.

Smoking cigarettes increases the risk of disease and debilitating health problems. But for Generation Risk, part of the *attraction of smoking* is its inherent risk. For this fast-paced generation, accustomed to immediate feedback and hungry for new sources of stimulation, emphasizing even the most graphic and devastating health risks of smoking doesn't help, because teenagers don't relate to long-term consequences.

To get through to Generation Risk, parents have to be ready for a no-hypocrisy regime of honest talk. Parents have to be willing to listen. Parents have to get at root causes, and then empower their teenagers to make their own choices. *They will anyway,* with or without parental input.

This book is not simply based on personal opinion or informed judgment. The information presented in this book is supported by a wide range of documented research, both academic and scientific; the knowledge and experience of experts in a variety of fields related to teenagers; the expertise of public health professionals; and opinions of teenagers themselves.

Specifically, I've drawn information from every source I could muster, both inside my company and outside. I've interviewed company research scientists about the technical aspects of cigarettes and tobacco, and I've made a comprehensive study of our own company documents.

I've sat for three years on the Executive Committee of Brown & Williamson Tobacco Corporation, the highest decision-making body of the company. As the corporate officer responsible for reviewing all marketing programs for the company to be sure they are not targeted at youth, I've researched the impact of advertising and promotion on youth smoking.

I've met with physicians and health education leaders and studied published reports on smoking and disease. I've conducted interviews with professionals who work with children, social psychologists, and experts in the field of risk and protective factors. I've reviewed technical studies on smoking, addiction, and disease, and I've observed focus group sessions among hundreds of teenagers, as well as parents, teachers, and counselors.

I've listened for dozens of hours to teenagers talking about themselves and the challenges they face: about smoking, about friendship, about parents, about violence, about trust, and about growing up. I've listened to parents, teachers, and counselors discuss teenage issues and share their views about risk behavior, discipline, the role of the school, and the importance of parental involvement.

The research referenced in this book was conducted in Dallas, Louisville, Miami, Boston, St. Louis, San Francisco, Philadelphia, Los Angeles, Denver, Atlanta, Chicago, New Orleans, and Roanoke, and represents an economically and racially diverse mix of teenagers and adults with surprisingly similar anxieties and perspectives about teenage risk.

As a mother, I've felt an overpowering surge of emotions engulf me when my children were at risk. As my children have progressed through their teenage years, I've swelled with pride and elation as they've learned and achieved, shared the sadness of their disappointments, felt the flashing anger of their frustrations, and suffered a hollow churning of anxiety over their safety. I've nurtured them, disciplined them, loved them, and, at times, I failed them. I've thought deeply about our relationships, about the awesome responsibility of parenting, and about what's worked for me as a parent in the age of Generation Risk.

Throughout my thirty-year career in business, I've learned how to solve certain problems with head-on determination, and how to handle others with a mixture of sensitivity and finesse. I know how to negotiate agreements, analyze information, evaluate options, and make decisions. I understand that when the stakes are high, we can find ways of overcoming obstacles, accelerating timetables, and developing breakthrough ideas. *These are the kinds of skills parents need* to communicate effectively with their teenagers.

As a tobacco executive dedicated to preventing youth smoking, I've encountered skepticism, rejection, and outright hostility. To many people, the job of keeping teenagers from smoking cigarettes is hopeless. Still others assume that anything that comes from a tobacco executive must be bad.

But this book is *not a defense of tobacco companies*. This book is *not pro-tobacco*. This book is borne from a deep understanding of tobacco and its attraction to teenagers, and a fervent personal commitment to help parents keep their teenagers from smoking.

As one demonstration of that commitment, all proceeds from this book will be donated to programs to prevent youth smoking.

But even the best public programs will never compare to the strength and importance of a parent's influence over a teenager's well-being. The most powerful protective factors in a teenager's life are self-esteem and family bonds, *and it's up to parents to help protect their teenagers from risk.*

Part I of this book will deepen your understanding of teenage risk-taking, peer pressure, and the impact of popular culture. Part II will show you new ways to strengthen your relationship with your teenager through trust, respect, and responsibility. Part III will help you understand smoking, and help you empower your teenager to repel the threats that assault and entice Generation Risk.

As one concerned and caring parent to another, I offer you the ideas in this book to help your vulnerable, precious, wonderful teenager.

—Corky Newton

ACKNOWLEDGMENTS

THANKS FIRST AND MAINLY to my husband Lowell, whose special attitude and unparalleled love and support could never be matched. I will always remember the inspiration and resolve that welled up inside me when I told him how I planned to approach this project. "Why are you wasting your time on that?" he asked. "Parents can't tell *teenagers* anything!" He was right, so this book is not about "telling."

Next I'd like to thank my friends, who have provided support and perspective over the years and especially during times of stress: Trina, Sharon, Rhoda, Cathy, Susie, Theresa, Linda, Eleanor, Joan, Maggie, Lucy, Sherry, Pam, Carla, Charlie, and Barbara. Thanks to my counselors and advisors for your encouragement and assistance: John, Dan, Amy, Jodie, Jim, Marcie, Brendan, and Joe.

Thanks to Nick, for your confidence and commitment.

Thanks to Gloria, who taught me to love metaphors and other wondrous things.

A special thanks to my friend Bonnie McCafferty, who can do anything and who proves that the value of positive feedback never ends.

Thanks to Kate Kelly, for your sense of clarity and organization.

Thanks especially to Bob Levine, who believed in this book and the good it could do from the beginning, and to my editor, Marc Baller, whose critical feedback, support, and encouragement have made this book measurably better.

Thank you to my adorable sister Kerri, to her husband Jerry, and to my dear Mom, who's always on my side regardless of the situation. Thanks to my brother Bucky, who taught me all about sibling rivalry, baseball, and competition.

More than anything, thank you to my terrific kids, Natalie and Ted, and to our dog Fergie, all of whom I love and appreciate more than chocolate itself.

PART I

UNDERSTANDING TEENAGERS AND RISK

1

TEENS WHO SMOKE, AND WHY THEY DO

Jason is a teenage smoker. He lives with his mother and his two younger sisters. His mother is a nurse who works late many evenings and often on weekends. At age sixteen, Jason is tired of being saddled with responsibilities for babysitting his sisters, who don't listen to him anyway. He wants to be left alone instead of being constantly hassled by his mother about cleaning up, doing homework, and everything else she can dream up.

Jason has been home from school for about three hours. The dishes from dinner are still on the table next to his books. The girls are watching television. As he sinks back into a chair to relax and pulls a pack of cigarettes from his pocket, his mother walks in and starts in on him.

"Jason, how can you smoke? We've talked about this so many times before! You know you're risking lung cancer or heart disease or emphysema."

None of Jason's friends have lung cancer, heart disease, or emphysema. He has heard this speech before, and it means nothing to him. He doesn't plan to smoke forever. He tunes his mother out and begins to daydream. He holds the pack in his right hand and pulls off the thin gold tear tape with his left. The tape always comes off perfectly, always in one piece. He leaves the cellophane on the bottom of the pack because he likes the way it feels in his fingers, and he likes to hear that soft crackle every time he takes the pack out of his pocket.

His mother is harping at him again; *"Do you want to die from lung cancer?"*

Jason immerses himself in the ritual of opening the pack. He flips open the box with his thumb and pulls away the loose foil covering the cigarettes. There they are: two tightly packed rows of cork-tipped cigarettes, just waiting for him to pick one out.

His mother is going on; *"Don't you know you're ruining your lungs?"*

Jason pulls a cigarette out of the pack and sticks it in his mouth as he snaps the box closed. He lets the cigarette hang between his lips while he drops the pack back into his pocket. It feels good there. And he knows he looks good. He reaches into his pocket for the lighter.

His mother's voice drifts in and out; *". . . kills over 400,000 people a year. . . ."*

The lighter is in Jason's right hand. The cigarette is still hanging between his lips. He doesn't hold the cigarette with his fingers to light it. Girls do that. He's happy now. Man, he really wants to smoke. He snaps his lighter, and the flame engulfs the end of the cigarette. He loves that. He especially loves it in the dark. The cigarette ignites. The tobacco crinkles evenly all around the tip. He inhales deeply and drops the lighter back into his pocket. Ah, there it is now. That sharp rasp on the soft tissue at the back of the throat. The smoke feels like silk in his mouth. His lungs are full. Now the satisfying exhale. He blows the smoke out in a straight stream and watches it swirl in the air.

"Jason, how can you just ignore me when I'm trying to protect you from something dangerous and harmful?"

Jason is waiting now to flick the ashes. He likes to watch them come off the end of the cigarette cleanly. He takes another long, satisfying drag.

"Have you even thought about what you're doing to your body by smoking cigarettes?"

Jason blocks out her words and immerses himself in a feeling of tranquility as he inhales again. Now he's almost reached the end of the cigarette. One last drag to finish it off. Last chance to smoke for awhile, so it's got to be a big puff to linger with him.

His mother's exasperated voice breaks through, *"What does it take to get through to you, anyway?"*

He finally answers, *"You don't have a clue, do you, Mom?"*

Perhaps you recognize Jason. He may live in your home or that of your neighbor. He started smoking at a young age and, by now, he is as sophisticated in his smoking habit as any adult. What can Jason's mother (or you) ever do to convince him that he's too young to smoke, that he shouldn't be smoking at all?

Or perhaps your teenager is more like fourteen-year-old Amanda. She would never light up in front of you, yet after she has been out with her friends on the weekend, she returns home and, under the fresh scent of perfume she must have sprayed on her clothes, you detect something else. You hope the musty smell of smoke is just from being around other kids who are smoking, but you wonder. . . .

Wearing a bright pink halter top and ragged cutoff jeans, Amanda is talking to her guidance counselor, whom she likes and trusts: *"There are certain things you just don't want to tell your parents because you don't want to hurt them. You don't want them to be disappointed in you,"* she says. Amanda is twisting back and forth in her chair, looking mostly at the floor. She leans forward and wrinkles her brow as she looks up at her counselor.

"But your friends are really important to you. You want to try and fit in with everybody so sometimes you experiment and go do what other people are doing. I don't know. Sometimes it's really hard to know what to do."

Like so many other teens, Amanda is tempted to try a cigarette. She is uncomfortable about the idea of deceiving her parents, but she wants to fit in with her friends and doesn't want to miss anything that might be fun. What can you do to convince her not to smoke?

Or maybe neither a "Jason" nor an "Amanda" is on your mind right now. Maybe you're a smoker yourself, like Martina's mother. You know the pleasurable aspects of smoking that could attract a teenager (the calming effect, the routine, the enjoyable taste, the comfort of having something to do with your hands besides eat, and so on.) But you also know the negatives (the odor that permeates everything, the feeling of doing something you can't easily control, and the long-term concerns about health), and you don't want your teenager to follow in your footsteps. How do you convince your teen to "Do as I say, not as I do?"

Martina is only twelve years old and answers questions freely and easily. Her youthful face is framed with bouncy curls, and she seems to be bursting with energy. The summer sun has bleached her hair and lightly freckled her face.

"My mom smokes, but she always tells my sister and me, 'Don't smoke because it's not good for you.'" Wearing a yellow T-shirt, red shorts, and thick-soled tennis shoes, she cocks her head to the side when she talks. "I'm like, 'Well, you're telling us not to do something that you've done all your life, and you're still doing it.' She's like, 'Well, I learned from my mistake, and I'm trying to help you so you don't make the same one.'"

"It's really confusing to know what to do because, you know, I'm curious what it's like."

Jason's, Amanda's, and Martina's parents face a problem confronting all parents today: how to communicate with teenagers about the long-range (and not so long-range) dangers of some of their behaviors. To a teenager, invincibility is part of his personality makeup, and because smoking, complete with its forbidden "label," provides short-term thrills, excitement, and immediate gratification, teens see little reason to refrain from trying it. Long-term consequences are not relevant because teenagers are oblivious to their own mortality.

As a parent, the issue facing you is to find ways to help your kids avoid risky behavior instead of seeking it. The task ahead of you is not an easy one. And, in the case of smoking in particular, the attractions for teenagers are strong.

THE MYSTIQUE OF SMOKING

What is the mystique about cigarettes that tempts so many teenagers to try smoking before they are even fifteen? Parents seeking simple answers to this complex question will encounter only frustration and disappointment. The reasons go beyond rule breaking, emulation of movie star role models, curiosity, and the desire to take a risk. The smoking experience encompasses a network of interconnected physical, social, and psychological factors that can intrigue and attract teenagers.

Why People Smoke

Smokers describe the effects of smoking in terms of taste and flavor, and talk about "impact"—the split-second sensation that smoke produces in the back of their throats, something like the bubbly stimulation of carbonation in soft drinks, something to anticipate and savor.

Cigarettes provide a whole range of sensations to satisfy smokers, and the smoking experience involves far more than simply the physical effects. There are social dimensions to smoking that complicate and enhance the ritual, and perhaps most importantly, psychological aspects that affect the smoker's self-image.

Cigarette smoking is a unique experience that represents a jumble of contradictions. Smokers *love* cigarettes and *hate* cigarettes. Cigarettes can be both *stimulating* and *relaxing*. Cigarettes taste *terrible* and *wonderful*. Cigarettes help people feel *more comfortable in social situations*, and yet many smokers feel *socially ostracized*.

If all the effects of smoking were negative, it would be a lot easier to convince teenagers not to smoke. But because the smoking experience is also gratifying, the obstacles are tougher. Teenagers see smoking as a form of self-indulgence, and they feel entitled to a share of the pleasure.

It's a compelling fact that *many people like to smoke*. In marketing research studies, smokers list a number of reasons why they smoke:

- It's relaxing.
- I like the taste.
- It has a calming effect.
- It's part of a routine that I'm used to.
- It gives me something to do with my hands.
- It makes drinking more enjoyable.
- It adds to my enjoyment of a meal.
- It keeps my weight down.
- It helps me feel at ease with people I don't know.

- It helps me concentrate.
- It helps keep me awake.

Social psychologists and health researchers have determined that, for teenagers, there are even more reasons:

- It's against the rules.
- My friends do it.
- It makes me look older.
- It's a cool thing to do.

Judith Rich Harris, author of *The Nurture Assumption*, believes that "it is because adults don't approve of smoking—because there is something dangerous and disreputable about it—that teenagers want to do it."

The Sensation of Smoking

The smoking experience is multifaceted and unique to each smoker. Even though beginning smokers typically react negatively to the taste and impact of their first cigarettes, smokers often develop a desire to experience the wide range of sensory reactions to cigarettes.

For example, smokers expect and want a certain degree of "irritation" when they smoke, almost a slightly painful sensation in the throat, mouth, or chest. Without irritation, the cigarette tastes bland or "blah" and feels like inhaling hot air.

As smoke enters the mouth, it triggers taste sensations—good tobacco taste or bad tobacco taste, good or bad menthol taste. Smokers savor just the right feel of the smoke in the mouth to enhance the smoking experience. If there is too little, they complain that the cigarette is too hard to draw or too meek or mild. If there is too much smoke, they say it is harsh, strong, or irritating.

Smokers describe the "body" of the smoke, which is the weight of the smoke in the mouth. More body means more substance, more richness, more fullness, like the difference between a milkshake and a glass of milk. Smokers are concerned about "smoothness"—the amount of tobacco taste, the absence of a jarring sensation. For menthol cigarettes, they expect a "cooling effect"—a refreshing rush of flavor like the feeling of sucking air after eating a peppermint candy, and a tingling sensation in the mouth.

Another big part of smoking is anticipation. Smokers expect to be satisfied, calmed, yet stimulated.

The Look and Feel

Smokers like to watch smoke swirling in the air. It's relaxing to see the stream of exhaled smoke dissipate into gentle wisps. The deep breathing associated with smoking is, in itself, a calming experience and a stress reliever.

Smokers like the feel of the pack in their hands, the sound of the cellophane outer wrapping, and the aroma of the cigarette tobacco and flavorings when they open the pack. They like to feel the texture of the cigarette paper in their hands and on their lips. They like to flick the ashes and to stub out the cigarette in a certain way as an expression of smoking style: smashing out the lit end, folding the cigarette over the stubbed out end, rolling the burning tip out of the end, or partially extinguishing the lit end to let the cigarette smolder in the ashtray.

Smoking to Lose Weight

Researchers in Boston have recently established that the desire to lose weight is another important reason why some kids smoke. As reported by the Associated Press, Dr. Alison Field of Harvard Medical School noted that "girls who were unhappy with their appearance were twice as likely to think about using tobacco," and that "those who were doing something to lose weight were more likely to smoke than those who were not."

Weight is a sensitive subject for teenagers. Researchers in the study asked only indirect questions about weight and smoking because they didn't want to suggest to kids that smoking could help them lose weight. Dr. Michael Jellinek, chief of child psychiatry at Massachusetts General Hospital, pointed to the "societal stereotype of being very thin" as a motivation for teenagers to take health risks to lose weight.

Hollywood isn't helping. A recent *People* magazine cover story challenged the wisdom of supermodels, actors, dancers, and stars who starve themselves to fit the latest trend in skinny shapes, risking infertility and osteoporosis to maintain their single-digit dress sizes.

For teenagers highly susceptible to influences from role models, the concept of taking health risks to look thin may seem perfectly acceptable.

Stacked against these attributes about smoking is a formidable list of things smokers *dislike* about cigarettes. But for smokers the negatives can all be overcome, rationalized away, or postponed. The social, physical, and psychological aspects of smoking form a powerful combination. So this list of negatives—the primary source of logic for antismoking advocates—has little chance of dissuading a determined smoker:

- Smoking increases my risk of disease.
- Cigarettes are expensive.
- I feel too dependent on cigarettes.
- The ashes are messy.
- I sometimes burn my clothes with the ashes.
- There's an unpleasant aroma in my clothes, the room, or my car.
- They make my throat feel scratchy.
- They fill the air with smoke.
- They leave stains on my teeth and fingers.
- They give me bad breath.
- When I smoke, I run out of breath easily.
- They leave an unpleasant aftertaste.
- They annoy other people.

For teenagers bent on making their own decisions, the standard arguments have even less effect.

WHY OLD SOLUTIONS DON'T WORK

Humpty Dumpty sat on a wall;
Humpty Dumpty had a great fall;
All the King's horses and all the King's men
Couldn't put Humpty together again.
*So the King said, "Then I want **more** horses, and **more** men!"*

This parody of the well-known Humpty Dumpty nursery rhyme is both funny and ironic. When the King dedicated all of his resources toward putting Humpty together, he failed. His defeat stemmed from the fact that

Humpty Dumpty was an egg, who could not be put back together through the force of horses and men. The joke is funny because it is so obvious that *more of the wrong solution* will not solve the problem. It's sad because that's the way we often behave ourselves.

When faced with problems that confront our teenagers, we naturally apply logic. When that doesn't work, we apply more logic.

Like Jason's mother and many parents like her, health organizations continue to drum into kids the dangers of smoking. That's symptomatic of the natural knee-jerk reaction most people display when faced with the issue of youth smoking. They tell kids that cigarettes cause lung cancer, heart disease, emphysema, and other diseases, and are responsible for over 400,000 deaths a year. They show pictures of people who have contracted these diseases. They show pictures of diseased organs. They describe the long-term consequences.

For decades, parents have used the expression, "If I've told you once, I've told you a thousand times . . ." But if the child has already heard a warning/admonition/threat a thousand times, and has failed to heed it, why say it again?

This type of behavior (repeating warnings that have never worked before) is particularly ineffective with teenagers who are challenging adult authority and wisdom at every opportunity. In this context, appeals to long-term thinking are bound to fail, particularly with a generation which is growing up in a world of instant access through cell phones, pagers, e-mail, and faxes. If teenagers can't taste it, feel it, wear it, or drive it—*now*—they can't relate to it. They've never had to wait for anything. To influence this fast-paced and sensory-overloaded generation, reasons for avoiding risks must have relevance, impact, and immediacy.

If the approach of emphasizing the health risks of smoking and the dangers of other types of risky behavior hasn't worked with teenagers yet, more of the same is not likely to help. So what will? That's what you'll learn later on in the book.

First, it's important to understand that smoking doesn't occur in isolation. Teenagers push what they perceive to be the limits in many aspects of their lives. If your teenager is smoking, that may be only one of a number of risky behaviors. To best guide your teenager, you can begin by understanding this generation's compelling desire to take risks.

HIGH RISK LIVING—A NEW CULTURAL NORM

Teenagers today have grown up with R-rated movies, explicit language in rap music, plenty of money, and essentially free access to all varieties of indulgences.

The world they see is one where adults are already living life on the edge. While our own parents may have pursued traditional pastimes such as baseball, reading, motor boating, gardening, or golf, we as parents have peers who are already pushing life's limits.

We see millions of adult Americans engaging with a passion in sporting activities so exhilarating, dangerous, and thrilling that they have been dubbed "extreme sports"—snowboarding, mountain biking, ice-climbing, paragliding, skateboarding, and jumping off cliffs over rushing waters with small single chutes. Unprotected sex is raging, and the popularity of heroin is surging as a drug of choice among the chic. Day trading in stocks has usurped long-term conservative investment. Venture capital and high-tech firms dominate new trends in business school graduate employment.

If *adults* are taking these kinds of risks, what's left for kids who want to rebel to establish their independence?

Additional risk, of course. In order to forge a path of their own, these teens feel the solution is to push the limits on not just one front, but on as many as seem fun on any given Friday night or Tuesday afternoon. As a result, this generation—your teenager's peer group—is defining a new paradigm of interaction with parents and teachers, treating home as a place for refueling and school as an obstacle course in risk exposure to drinking, smoking, drugs, violence, and sex.

As these teenagers break free from parental control to establish independence, they are engaging in risk behaviors of a new order of magnitude. For this generation, mildly offensive acts to shock their parents are not enough. They are displaying a startling degree of sophistication, independence, and boldness as they smoke, drink, pierce and tattoo their bodies, and experiment with drugs. If they want something, they can find it *and get it* on the Internet. They have been weaned on MTV and extreme sports, and they *love risk*.

Even teenagers who may not pierce body parts or dabble with drugs are not afraid to try smoking, and most are relatively open about it despite parental disapproval.

To protect your teenager from smoking and other dangerous behavior, you must first understand what drives today's savvy, adventurous, modern teenagers whose attitudes of boldness and invincibility have branded their generation with a new title and a new identity: *Generation Risk.*

If you really don't want *your* teenager to smoke, you need to do more than disapprove. You can't leave it up to the schools to protect your teenager. You have to get personally involved, and you have to know what you're talking about. You have to understand why teens take risks, and why they pick smoking as a badge of defiance.

2

RISK-TAKING AND ITS APPEAL TO YOUR TEENAGER

Teenagers are individuals, each with a unique set of motivations, family circumstances, friendships, experiences, and psychological forces alternately accelerating and slowing their social development. Each person enters the teenage transition period as a child and leaves it transformed by a storm of physical and emotional changes.

For a parent, the maturation period for your teenager can represent times of turmoil and stress as you struggle to maintain contact with the newly emerging personalities, values, and identities that characterize your not-quite-adult child. You need to forge a new relationship with your teenager as the dependencies of the past are replaced by demands for freedom and independence.

The teen who lives with you probably shares common characteristics with other teenagers, whose new personality developments are destined to confound and frustrate parents. During these years, teens may be demanding, defensive, and disrespectful as well as contrary, confused, and conflicted. They are likely to be rowdy and rebellious, and to be willing to take risks as part of the normal process of growing up. Teenagers have to find ways to break away from parents to establish their independent identities, and rebelling against the rules is a common and expected practice. In addition to trying cigarettes, teens are tempted by any number of possibilities ranging from a slightly rebellious change of hair color to the more serious body piercings and the dangerous practices of drinking to excess or trying illicit drugs.

The more we as parents can understand about why teenagers take risks, the better chance we'll have of building a relationship that will help us guide them through these dangerous years safely.

RISK-TAKING:
A NORMAL PART OF GROWING UP

Risk-taking and rebellion are certainly not unique to the current generation of teenagers. The expectation that the teen years will be troubled and difficult times is well ingrained in our collective parental psyche. We can all remember taking risks as teenagers. Partly based on our own memories, we understand their motivation:

- Teens rebel to establish their independent identities.
- Teens feel invincible so risk-taking is less frightening to them.
- Teens want to fit in; if their friends are taking risks, they will, too.

This spirit of independence and desire for freedom from rules is demonstrated by many types of rebellious behavior, a few of which were listed in a March 1999 survey in *Teen* magazine:

BOYS
- Broke a car window for fun.
- Skipped school.
- Took the car without asking.
- Went skating at midnight.

GIRLS

- Stayed out past curfew.
- Drove 80 mph.
- Lied to parents.
- Egged an enemy's house.

For boys and girls alike, there's an implicit expectation that a few rules should be broken as a demonstration of spirit and self-confidence. We're not surprised or shocked to hear of teenagers who rebel in what we hope are harmless ways. We can relate to teenagers who seem to be crying out for independence and adventure.

What Teens Say About Risk

To help us better understand how to keep teens from pushing the limits too far, it seems ideal to consult the true "authorities," the teenagers themselves. Teenagers, eager to experience life, describe risk-taking as a normal part of the maturing process. They believe they are entitled to take part in everything they can reach, and they seize chances to test their speed and endurance.

Brittany

Brittany is twelve years old. Her head is blossoming with curly brown hair only partially held back by a row of barrettes that reveals a shining slice of her youthful, exuberant face. She is tugging at the hem of her overall jumper skirt to pull it down over her thigh as she wiggles into her chair. It seems to Brittany that she has been waiting forever to become a teenager so that she will be old enough for a few privileges. She sees older classmates dating, attending unchaperoned parties, smoking, and drinking beer. She doesn't want to disappoint her parents, but she wants to fit in with her friends.

"Sure I'm going to take some risks as a teenager. Risk and growing up are connected. They're together. As you grow older, you want to experience more things. It's like steps. I feel like, if you're going to get in trouble, go ahead and have all your fun while you're out there. I'm going to live my life to the fullest."

Justin

Justin's attitude about risk is pretty matter-of-fact. He's seen his two older brothers raise a lot of hell and never get into serious trouble. He's done a few things himself without major consequences, and at seventeen he thinks he can take care of himself. He's got his own rules for where to draw the line.

"I was going out with this one girl, and she always wanted to have sex. I mean, it was great, but—you don't know where that girl's been. Some guys skip school to be with their girlfriends, then they get high, then they have sex, so it's all three at once. It's easy to do whatever you want, really. Girls have sex in the back of the bus. It's an everyday thing. You just have to set your own rules for being careful."

Teenagers are not necessarily engaging in these activities as an outright expression of rebellion, but they are drawn to them as typical activities for people in their age group, and they mistakenly assume they can handle themselves in nearly any situation.

Derrick

Derrick is fifteen and pays a lot of attention to his hair. He has dyed the top blonde and wears it cut short into a crew cut, but it is long on the sides and in back where it is dark brown. Derrick is a whiz at math; he claims his 'D' in English doesn't bother him because he thinks the assignments are stupid.

"Daily life is an adventure. Skipping school, sneaking out, speeding. It's all an adventure. All teenagers live for is pleasure. If I know I'm not supposed to go somewhere, I do it anyway. Like my friend's parents were going out of town, and I went to his house anyway."

"My Kids Don't Do Those Things . . ."

Though most parents expect their teenagers to take some risks, they would be surprised to know their kids are drinking, smoking, or using drugs. "I know Pete's kids drink; mine go to those parties, but they don't drink . . . They're good kids," they'll say. Parents feel they've made it clear to *their* kids that these risky behaviors are not acceptable. Some of us tell them explicitly, and others convey the message more subtly, but all parents intend to protect their children from danger. When we later find that our own teenager was involved in something we don't condone, it's shocking—we don't like learning that our own kids are taking these risks.

Parents sometimes assume that their own children are not "at risk" simply because they do not fall into one of the more vulnerable socioeconomic categories. But, in fact, all kids are at risk, and all parents should watch vigilantly for danger signals. Sarah, an honor student, is a good example of the exposure teenagers share:

Sarah

In addition to earning good grades, Sarah is a member of the Bluebells cheering squad. She has long brown hair, blue eyes, and a sweet smile. Her parents are sure that she has never tried drugs, and that she would never consider smoking cigarettes. Her parents are wrong.

"It's fun because you get that rush, the excitement that you're doing something that everybody would say 'no' to. You're kind of being rebellious. You're experiencing new things, being your own person. You know the consequences, but you don't know if it's going to happen to you or not. It gives you an adrenaline rush. If you try something, and it actually works, then you're like, 'Oh my God! Wow!' That's what you're looking for."

The annual statistics gathered by the University of Michigan's Monitoring the Future Study show high rates of cigarette smoking, marijuana use, alcohol use, and inhalants among African-American, Hispanic, and Caucasian youth alike. Alcohol use (at least once within the last thirty days) among Hispanic kids is up to nearly 50 percent; cigarette use among Caucasian kids is over 40 percent; marijuana use among African-American kids is nearly 20 percent.

These are not just isolated problems. They affect all of our children, and as parents we need to watch carefully for signs of danger.

RECOGNIZING THE RISK-TAKERS

Brent

Brent's short dark hair is spiked rigidly upward on top of his head with styling gel, and his sideburns extend down to his jawline. Brent is seventeen and bored by most assignments his teachers give him. He sings in a rock band and might be able to cut a record soon. He is a talented tennis player, but erratic on the court. His quick temper and lack of respect for the coach have earned him a reputation for having a bad attitude.

"Why do teenagers take risks? To find out their boundaries. For fun. They want to go out and get high for the fun. Fun's the best thing you can have. You don't want to feel bad. If it makes you feel better, you're going to do it. I know my Dad doesn't want me to get drunk, but what's he going to do, kick me out? Let him."

Many teenagers seem to be daring their parents to force them to conform. Their rebellion is an expression of contempt for the rules. For others, casual risk-taking can result just from boredom with everyday routines.

Candice

Candice is a high school sophomore with long blonde streaked hair, pouty lips, and deep brown eyes. She is wearing white shorts and a bright orange tank top. Her socks are horizontally striped black and orange, and her feet are enveloped in clunky black tennis shoes with thick white soles. She looks like a large bumblebee.

"I don't do things purposely to get into trouble. I don't try to do bad things, just to go against the rules. I just fall into some things. But most of the time I do what my parents ask because I respect them and don't want to disappoint them. When I argue with my parents, it's about little things like minor disagreements or something."

Brent and Candice are both encountering a series of challenges and temptations as they work through their high school years. They are both searching for independence and freedom. One is openly rebellious and isn't afraid to say so to himself or anyone else. The other is expressing her individuality through her choices of clothes and hairstyle that are well within the range of acceptability to her parents.

Which teenager is likely to try cigarettes, alcohol, or illegal drugs? *Both of them.*

Recent national studies on youth risk behavior show that huge percentages of high school-aged kids have participated in risky behaviors:

- 79.1 percent of students have had at least one drink of alcohol during their lifetime.
- 70.2 percent of students have tried cigarette smoking.
- 47.1 percent of students have used marijuana.
- 31.7 percent of students have been offered, sold, or given an illegal drug *on school property* during the last year.
- 48.4 percent of students have had sexual intercourse.

BUT WHY?

If you discover condoms in your son's or daughter's dresser drawer or a pack of cigarettes in the backpack, or if it's your teenager who comes stumbling home drunk from what was supposed to be a supervised party, you're going to be angry, hurt, and very unsettled about what to do. What happened to that child who used to love to go to movies, hang out with the family, and enjoy few things more than telling you all the details of a day at school?

What is it about risk that appeals so strongly to the teenagers of this generation?

It's a Rush, and My Parents Would Never Let Me Do It

Teenagers explain that one of their key reasons for taking risks is the sheer exhilaration and sense of adventure involved. Part of the enjoyment for teenagers comes from the fact that they're breaking rules. Another level of tension layered on top of the danger itself is the risk of being caught by parents.

For teenagers struggling to define themselves as individuals, risk-taking and rebellion can serve as a pair of crowbars to pry them free of parental control.

Jennifer

Jennifer has been painting her toenails while waiting for her interview to begin. The nails are now a bright shade of blue, with sparkles built into the nail polish, and she takes frequent peeks at her sandaled feet as she speaks, avoiding eye contact. She is chewing gum, and occasionally pokes her tongue through the glutinous mass to form an air bubble, then rolls it to her back teeth to make it smack as a punctuation mark to her opinions.

"I think a lot of people do things just because they're not supposed to. If something was allowed and if their parents didn't care what they were doing, then probably it wouldn't be that big a deal. But a lot of people smoke because they're not supposed to, and if their parents said, 'Go ahead and smoke,' they might not want to. But when it's forbidden or whatever, then it gives you a rush just to do it."

Not all teenagers engage in illegal or life-threatening activities, but it's natural for them to seek stimulating outlets for their energy and emotions. With so many choices available today, it's easy for kids to drift from one level of risk to another just to keep up the level of excitement.

Risk-taking is not confined to teenagers of any given social class or socioeconomic group. Economically disadvantaged kids with few opportunities to participate in organized, supervised after-school activities want to rebel against whatever rules have been imposed upon them, and they want to feel the rush of excitement that's inherent in taking risks. For middle-class kids with plenty of material possessions and access to entertainment, there's still an attraction to rule-breaking and risk-taking rooted in the struggle to become autonomous adults.

Jill

Jill lives in an upscale neighborhood and drives a pink Geo Tracker. Her clothes are carefully selected to show off her figure as well as their designer labels. Jill is looking at her reflection in the interview room mirror, which is really a viewing window for observers in the next room.

"In my school a lot of kids carry around their prescription medication. You mix it with alcohol and it makes you all crazy, then you're like, 'Wow.' What makes it fun is that your parents don't want you to do it, but they don't know. And if you really get out there on the edge, then there's a special thrill to it. My parents want me to just stay in this safety zone like a boring little robot. I mean, give me a break."

Because teenagers are extremely accepting of each other's behavior, they often shield their friends from parental scrutiny. Parties are organized as social activities but also as opportunities for teenagers to congregate and experiment as a group, far away from the eyes of their parents and regulated only by occasional proctoring by the adults who happen to live with the hosting teenager.

Kyle

Kyle's legs are growing so fast that he has to buy new jeans every few months to keep his ankles from showing. Kyle is a good student and plays on the junior varsity golf team. His father is a police officer and his mother works in a chiropractor's office. Kyle plans to go out and get wasted tonight after the game, then stay overnight with Brandon so his parents don't see him drunk.

"The whole partying scene is full of what you might call risks. There's always drinking and weed, and sometimes other drugs. Kids do it because they want to and because you're not supposed to do it. My parents would flip out, but you do it anyways."

Teenagers Feel Invulnerable

Kids are generally at their peak of physical condition during their adolescent years. They stay up late (or even all night) and still have boundless energy the next day. They race up and down soccer fields for hours, and are still ready to party at night. They run around outside in freezing weather without a coat but don't catch colds.

Teenagers stretch the limits of their endurance and impress themselves with their own resiliency. They routinely ignore the warnings of older, wiser, more experienced parents and reject common sense and caution in favor of sensory immersion. Each successive example of unpunished reckless chance-taking reinforces their misguided sense of insulation from harm.

Many kids just don't consider their risk-taking choices to be particularly serious. They talk about drugs, sex, or smoking as casually as we might talk about eating lunch. To parents, these risks sound not only serious, but seriously scary.

But because teens live so intensely in the present, they are concerned only about things that happen *now*, not things that might happen in the future. They typically feel young and strong, and think nothing harmful will happen to them. Teenagers are so focused on the moment that they don't think long-term.

Kevin

Kevin's natural hair color is red, and he has never liked it. Last month he dyed it bright green and carved a big K into his haircut. His left eyebrow is pierced with two rings.

"It's the typical teen intellect. Nothing is going to happen to me. It's like this I'm-on-top-of-the-world complex and nobody can touch me. I'm never going to die, and I can do this and this and this, and nothing is going to happen. We think we can do pretty much anything and not get in trouble for it. Like, 'Okay, let's do a little heroin.' It's like you're cheating death."

Because many of the negative consequences of life's choices are cumulative, most teens have never experienced them. They need tangible, personal experiences to help them internalize understanding. Somebody else's experiences may be mildly interesting to hear about, but *if someone else puts his hand in fire, I don't feel the pain.*

Teenagers simply haven't had a wide enough range of experience to help them relate to the long-term consequences of their actions. Therefore these outcomes are often blocked out, overshadowed by curiosity, or eclipsed by a general disdain for problems associated with aging. To many teenagers, the future is so far away that it is irrelevant.

Jennifer

Jennifer's toenails have dried, and she has turned her attention to her hair, which she is attacking vigorously with a collapsible nylon brush featuring small plastic bulb-like tips at the end of each bristle. As she strokes the brush through her long brown hair, she pulls her head backward and thrusts her chin forward and upward in an unconscious gesture. She looks like she is soaring down a mountainside on skis and feeling a rush of wind in her face.

"When you're a teenager, everybody is like, 'Oh, don't smoke, be smart.' You're just like, 'What happens if I smoke? I'm not going to die that second.' Pretty much everyone dies. If you develop cancer, by that time you're already sixty-five and gross-looking anyway."

The attitude of invincibility many teens exhibit is underscored by their consumer habits as they reject common sense and caution with impunity. Teenagers indulge in excessive behavior in the way they eat and shop. Generation Risk eats more snack foods and desserts than any other segment of the population. They spend more than $14.5 billion a year in fast food restaurants such as Pizza Hut, Wendy's, and Taco Bell. Yet as if nature has designed their bodies to counteract waves of reckless treatment, their high-energy activity levels make them far less likely to gain weight and develop high cholesterol than adults.

Stephanie

Stephanie is self-conscious about her height. At sixteen, she is taller than most of her friends, including the boys. She is wearing blue jeans and a tank top, and has her arms crossed over her chest and her head turned slightly to the side. Her long hair covers most of her face. She is not wearing any makeup. She is eating a Hershey bar and drinking a Mountain Dew.

"I think teenagers just want a challenge. Taking a risk is like, it's a challenge you overcome. Or curiosity. It gives us more experience in life. If we

don't do it, then we won't ever live, so we have to do it. You know smoking pot is bad for you, but you want to try it to see what it's like, you know. Knowing that smoking is a risk makes you want to try it. You want to know what happens. But you never think something bad is going to happen to you."

Teenagers feel invincible in part because they view risks as everyday events, as nothing out of the ordinary. They consider these activities to be just a standard part of the world in which they live, and they are curious about all its dimensions. They feel free to experiment and to explore.

Brian

Brian is a sophomore who has just moved to the suburbs with his family after living in an urban area of Chicago. He is wearing his cargo pants low over his hips so the top of his boxers shows when his T-shirt rides up. He narrows his eyes and glances nonchalantly at the interviewer.

"There's experimentation with all kinds of drugs. There's more drugs out there than most people know about. At my old school people carried deadly weapons, like—bombs and stuff. I know how to make Molotov cocktails. A lot of my friends are into every drug: cocaine, marijuana, acid. It starts in the third grade—real early. Almost everybody I know drinks and does drugs, but not the hard stuff like heroin. They smoke weed on the weekends or do whatever. I don't see a problem with that as long as you don't do anything stupid."

The feeling of invulnerability that many teenagers experience is particularly dangerous because it overcomes logic. Teenagers think they are in control when in fact they are teetering on the edge of risks with potentially catastrophic consequences. How many thousands of parents have issued the heartfelt warning, "Be careful," as their teenagers left for an evening out with friends? And how many teenagers have ignored that warning as they were swept up in the powerful tide of peer group influence?

PEER PRESSURE IS A POWERFUL INFLUENCE

Teenagers want to fit in with their friends. The need to belong to a group is a powerful drive for most adolescents, and the power of the peer group intensifies as the natural impulses to break away from parents increase.

Theresa

Theresa understands what it's like to want to fit in. She moved to a new school this year and was forced to find a whole new set of friends. At first it was really difficult and she hated her parents for dragging her to a new city. Then she found a group with whom she felt comfortable, and her life became bearable again.

"In my school, everybody has a group that you hang out with, just to be friends. You're just trying to fit in. It's just like at my old school. I was part of a group there, and I tried a drug. I mean, when I started it was because my friends were doing it."

The embarrassment of standing out from the group can drive teenagers to go along with behaviors they might not choose on their own. The old adage about boys and groups may well apply to teenagers even more strongly: "One boy, one brain. Two boys, half a brain. Three boys, no brain at all."

When teenagers get together, risk-taking abounds and good judgment is often abandoned.

The life stage called adolescence, which spans the years from about eleven to eighteen, has been indicted by numerous researchers as a breeding ground for risk behaviors. The virus that infects our well-behaved, affectionate, sensible children and transforms them into reckless, belligerent strangers is called "peer pressure." The influence of peers is considered the single most important factor in determining when and how cigarettes are first tried. When teenagers smoke, they usually smoke together: 60 percent of eleven to seventeen year olds smoke with close friends—and twelve to fourteen year olds whose best friends smoke are four times more likely to be smokers themselves. Adolescence is a consistent predictor of smoking, because adolescence is when peer pressure establishes its insidious hold.

Probably the most famous experiment on peer pressure was conducted by social psychologist Solomon Asch in the late '40s and early '50s. Asch tricked subjects into revealing the power of peer pressure by asking them to participate in a simple experiment about visual perception. Students were asked to look at a line, then to identify which of several other lines matched it in length. The answers were obvious. When they worked alone, 99 percent of the subjects picked the correct match.

Then they were put into groups to answer the same sorts of questions, but only one student in each group was really a test subject. The others in each group periodically insisted that a shorter or longer line was really the correct match. In this context, 76 percent of the test subjects succumbed to the pressure of the group and selected an incorrect line at least once, even though the group response was clearly wrong.

Psychologists continue to explore the dynamics of peer pressure to understand why the attraction of peer identification increases as children grow and develop. Herbert Lingren, Extension Family Scientist at the University of Nebraska, explains that pre-adolescents undergoing rapid physical, emotional, and social changes naturally turn to friends for advice, and begin to question adult standards and the need for adult guidance.

Ben

Ben is a sophomore in high school and is tired from soccer practice. He wants to get home to call his girlfriend, but mostly he is thinking about the pizza that the interviewer promised will arrive any minute. Ben is slumping in his chair with his legs extended straight out and his arms wrapped over his chest. His baseball cap with a Notre Dame logo is pulled down almost over his eyes.

"It's like drinking or something. If your friends are doing it, you're not going to sit there and just look at the bottle. You're going to sip some. You're not going to be the only one sober when everyone else is drunk, so you might as well go ahead and do it. Everybody's gonna try something like smoking a cigarette or taking a drink."

Generation Risk is not the first group of teenagers to feel the influence of peer pressure. What *is* new is the standard of behavior that defines peer acceptance, and the availability of risk.

They Have Access

Every one of the fifty states has a law against selling cigarettes to minors. The minimum drinking age nationwide is twenty-one. *Teenagers know* that marijuana, cocaine, heroin, PCPs and crystal meth (methamphetamine) are illegal drugs.

But teenagers also know that if they want to find cigarettes, alcohol, or drugs, they don't have to look far. Over 70 percent of teenagers report that they buy their own cigarettes, and if they can't buy them personally, their friends will do it for them. If these kids want to engage in dangerous risks, it's not difficult to find opportunities.

Cesar

Cesar is built like a fireplug: low to the ground and solid as concrete. He has dark eyes and hair, and is wearing a muscle shirt and tight-fitting pants. He seems more physically mature than the other kids in the group standing just outside the doorway, but he is only fourteen.

"We have the access. Right now, I can go get anything you need. I can get guns or whatever you want, and it shouldn't be like that. If you want a quart, you can go get one. If you need a car, you can go get one. I know where you can make one phone call and get a gun or get some drugs."

Programs to enforce access laws in retail stores are important, but they can't stop teenagers who are determined to get around the rules. As a demonstration of one way to outsmart the system, WBZ News recently reported that teenagers in Boston showed their congressman just how easy it was to order cigarettes from the Internet. They found twenty-six Web sites that sold cigarettes, none of them exhibiting the Surgeon General's warning about harmful effects of tobacco. Only half the sites had any language regarding age restrictions, and they were easily bypassed.

Sharif

Sharif is fifteen and loves to surf the Internet. He plans to start his own Internet company and become a millionaire before he is twenty-one. Sharif doesn't think it makes much sense to postpone his life just because his age profile doesn't happen to fit the rules somebody else designed for going to school, working, then retiring. He expects to retire before he is thirty and spend his time driving racecars and sipping wine.

"It's no problem to get booze or cigarettes. You can get a fake ID on the Internet any time. It takes about five minutes. Or you can get one of your friends to get it for you. Everybody has friends who are old enough to buy, and they'll help you out if you ask. Or go to a gas station around here. They'll sell you smokes without even asking. The age limit is a joke."

THE LAUNCH PAD

Teenagers take risks for understandable reasons. Just by virtue of being teenagers, they are barraged with a constant stream of opportunities, dares, and self-imposed pressures to push themselves and test the rules. In this sense today's teenagers are no different from generations of the past.

Yet something new defines the boundaries of current teenage behavior. Their early exposure to technology, advertising media, violence in movies and on television, and free access to material goods build a foundation of sophistication that no generation has ever before experienced. Their attitudes toward life are consistently more demanding and more adventurous than their predecessors. These are the issues we'll explore in the next chapter. The world our kids are growing up in is very different from the one you and I experienced, and it's important to understand how this new environment affects our teens.

Our teenagers are propelling themselves into orbit like rockets from a launch pad, exceeding the speed of sound and ignoring the established rules of the universe with space-age boldness. They are exploring a new theory of relativity, with risk as the variable.

3

THE SPECIAL
CHALLENGES OF TODAY

Every generation faces a unique set of challenges, and today's teenagers encounter risk as an everyday event. These kids have been exposed at early ages to adult themes on cable TV, uncensored language in music lyrics, and easy access to dangerous activities. Instead of the traditional family unit in which their parents were probably raised, Generation Risk is growing up in families comprised of single parents, second marriages, and all types of custody arrangements. Since 1980, the percentage of working mothers with teenagers has escalated from 64 percent to 80 percent. *One-fourth of teenagers live in single parent homes, up 80 percent from 1970.* Teenagers are regularly presented with temptations and opportunities in school and over long, unsupervised expanses of after-school hours. Even teenagers from traditional families are more mobile than ever before and have hours every day of unstructured, unsupervised time—time when risk-taking is among the options of "something to do."

MORE SERIOUS RISKS TODAY

The frightening aspect of what is happening today is that teenagers are flirting with more serious risks than previous generations ever encountered. A large number of teenagers go well beyond the relatively harmless list of misdemeanors commonly acknowledged in the past and are involved in dangerous risk-taking. Many teenagers who smoke, drink, or use marijuana don't consider these behaviors to be particularly risky.

The increasing nonchalance about dangerous behavior among teenagers is illustrated by the results of regional and national surveys that report trends in risk behavior and teenage attitudes. When the Monitoring the Future Study asked high school students about risk, the responses showed a surprising and alarming lack of concern by the students. Among twelfth graders, for example, only 61 percent of students said it was a great risk to try heroin once or twice without using a needle. *Heroin!* Only 63 percent of these kids said taking *four or five drinks nearly every day* was a great risk; only 57 percent for *taking barbiturates regularly;* only 69 percent for *smoking a pack or more of cigarettes a day.*

As parents, we should be worried that our teenagers are so blasé about activities we consider dangerous, and we should think critically about how these problems are being handled within the family as well as by schools and public health authorities. Unfortunately, it seems the climate is not changing for the better. The world that surrounds our children is filled with dangers, and their access to risks is becoming increasingly open.

Violence in and Out of Schools Is Increasing

When teenagers talk about their daily lives, they cite serious pressures. They speak of gangs, fights, and shootings as common occurrences. Many teens describe the violence and drugs in their worlds matter-of-factly, and without passing judgment. They seem to accept the growing violence in the world around them as an inevitable reflection of reality, and adjust their own behavior to blend with this jarring mosaic of anxiety and disorder.

A 1996 national teen violence survey reported that 47 percent of teens thought their schools were getting more violent, and 92 percent thought the world was getting more violent. Their opinions were more than impressions from a distance. Almost 30 percent of all teens, both boys and girls, reported engaging in at least one physical fight during the past year, and 37 percent (representing 8.4 million teens nationally) said that they knew someone who had been *shot*.

Violence has become the currency of respect in some schools. In order to prove worthiness, students are forced to fight. But the weapons of choice are more deadly than fists, and consequences of expressing unbridled anger are growing increasingly serious.

Shawn

Shawn is fifteen and attends a large public high school near his home. His coarse blonde hair is pulled back into a ponytail and knotted unevenly with a thick rubber band. He is dressed completely in black and is sporting a new tongue ring. He is practicing thrusting his tongue out to shock his teachers and friends at unexpected moments.

"In our school we have drugs. Mostly weed, sometimes acid, occasionally coke. Lots of people smoke. Certain kinds of kids use drugs—the more violent kids, that get stoned during lunch. We have fights, drugs, shootings. Somebody at our school got shot, over a girl of all things. The bloodstains are still on the sidewalk."

Experts speculate that television, movie, and video violence may contribute to the problem, predisposing teenagers to employ physical solutions to emotional problems, and desensitizing them from instinctive reactions to violence. *The American Academy of Pediatrics estimated in 1995 that, on average, children in this country will have viewed 200,000 acts of violence on television alone by age eighteen.*

Interactive video games have emerged as one of the most popular forms of adolescent entertainment, with revenues of $10 billion in the U.S. alone, or twice the amount Americans spend on attending movies. A 1993 study pegged "fantasy violence" and "human violence" as the most popular categories of video games, totaling 49 percent of player preferences.

Current editions of video games are astonishingly realistic, with sound effects including simulated cries of agony from on-screen victims. Players interact with these games from a first-person "shooter" perspective, looking through the sights of a weapon and shooting anything that moves, with no moral distinction between good guys versus bad. Maybe these video massacres are only games, but their profile fits perfectly with the hunger for stimulation and adventure exhibited by Generation Risk. Lt. Col. Dave Grossman, author of *On Killing: The Psychological Cost of Learning to Kill in War and Society,* warns of potentially lethal results, "The data on the effectiveness of simulators is overwhelming. And we're letting kids use murder simulators."

Carlos

Carlos is smaller than most of his friends, but he is wiry and tough. He is wearing a studded leather belt in his jeans and thick steel-toed black boots. At thirteen, Carlos is used to fighting and doesn't see anything wrong with his way of life. He is proud of the scars he carries on his hand from a knife fight last year.

"Everybody wants to start something. If you've been in a fight and you win, that's your respect, right there. A lot of people bring guns. If you get whooped enough, you're not going to take it no more. In sixth grade, there was this one boy who tried to take it out on me. He pushed me down the steps, and I fell. I got up, and I picked all my books up and everybody was laughing. He came down my street, talking about how he was going to beat me up, then I went in the house and got my bat, and broke his leg with my bat."

Some teenagers are afraid of the growing trends toward violence in and out of their schools. They regret that access to dangerous items is so open. They know that their peers are using drugs and carrying weapons.

D'Ron

D'Ron is twelve years old and has seen people killed in his neighborhood. His close-cropped hair, wide-open eyes, and smooth skin give him a look of innocence that sets him apart from the older boys in his class. Last week there was a drive-by shooting near his church, just at the time he usually walks past there from school. He doesn't want to get into trouble.

"When I was in fifth grade, somebody asked me to sell dope. I was walking home from school. I was scared, too, because when I walked past him, I didn't know, since I had said 'no,' if that dude would shoot me or not."

Researchers report that most teenagers believe alcohol and drugs are an important cause of violence in families and violence among young people. Faced with anxieties, pressures, and fears, some teenagers view cigarettes or alcohol as a form of escape. In the context of a violent world, lighting up to relax may seem to them to be a minor and insignificant risk.

The linkage between these risk behaviors is undeniably strong, and the reasons for addressing them at their roots are compelling.

They're Wired

Just as the day-to-day world our teens inhabit is filled with risks, so is the electronic world they can access in a couple of clicks. As the first generation to ride the wave of Internet technology, the teenagers of Generation Risk have access to unfiltered masses of information and an ability to connect with each other that creates powerful peer-level bonds and reinforces their sense of independence.

They've been called the "digital" or "wired" generation. These kids are computer literate, gaining and spreading information on the Internet and jumping from trend to trend with electronic speed. Being "wired" means being at home on the Web, understanding how to use computers for entertainment and self-gratification, and being connected. Many teenagers are never without their cell phones, pagers, answering services, or voice mail: they don't want to be out of the loop. There's a double meaning to the term "wired," too, that implies "flying high" either through the adrenaline rush of exciting activities or involvement with chemical stimulants.

Generation Risk stands for the rejection of moderation and head-first immersion in electronic shopping, international communications, and mass customization. These kids are accustomed to an overload of options and an extended network of peers who share their hunger for excitement.

We look at teenage behavior differently today because Generation Risk speaks the language of technology. A defining characteristic of this generation is their multimedia, multitasking capability. They simultaneously talk on the phone, surf the 'Net, listen to music, watch television, instant-message or chat on-line as standard operating procedure. Watching television while doing homework used to be considered a distraction. Today teenagers are empowering technology to activate all their senses at once, to heighten their ability to absorb information, and to pack multiple concurrent sensations into their realm of experience.

These teenagers have grown up with computers, and they have a technical fluency unmatched by any previous generation. With 500 television channels accessible by satellite dish, thousands of Internet Web sites, and a virtually unlimited selection of computer games vying for their attention, Generation Risk is inundated with options.

Over 60 percent of Generation Risk teenagers own compact disk players, 60 percent have cable TV, and 62 percent have their own personal computers. They have ready access to interactive kiosks and virtual reality.

They also have an unparalleled assault of marketing stimuli with which to contend. *Rolling Stone* magazine estimates these teenagers see as many as 400 ads per day.

Their exposure to marketing is no accident, according to *Business Week*. Marketers from McDonald's, Coca-Cola, and Universal Studios send out "street teams" of young recruits to hang out with teenagers in clubs, parks, and malls to gauge their interests and detect the latest trends. Delia's catalog for teenage girls thrives on electronically boosted grassroots support, spreading fashion fads by word of mouth and e-mail.

The importance of the Internet to Generation Risk is underscored by research that indicates a 50 percent increase in the number of teens online over a one-year period. Teenage boys say they spend less time sleeping because of the Internet, and they are watching less television.

The implications of the electronic age are staggering to parents struggling to influence this new generation of teenagers. Gradual stages of development for teenagers are a phenomenon of the past. Today's teenagers are connected to each other, to emerging market trends, to messages in music and film—with an immediacy that almost defies comprehension. As a parent, you have to contend with the Worldwide Web to get your teenager's attention.

They're Solvent

What else is different about these teenagers that sets them apart from their predecessors? *Their buying power.* Because of their collective size, their importance in the marketplace continues to increase. The teenage population is growing almost twice as fast as the total population. According to the U.S. Census Bureau, by the year 2010 there will be about 35 million teenagers in the U.S.

Many of the teenagers of Generation Risk are employed, and together they spent an estimated $141 billion in 1998. Most of the money teens have available to spend comes from their own earnings, with allowances representing less than half of their income. According to the U.S. Bureau of Labor Statistics, nearly half of the nation's teenagers have jobs, and one-fourth of all teenagers earn more than $100 per week.

Teenagers often equate financial freedom with true independence, and yearn to be out of school and on their own. With both parents working or a single parent working, kids are likely to be experienced in attending to their own basic needs. They indulge in nachos, pizzas, tacos, candy, and caffeine-loaded sodas, and supplement their spending money by working part-time in fast food restaurants or music stores, or selling electronic equipment on commission.

The spending clout of this generation of teenagers represents a significant market force. At Pacific Sunwear, a sports clothes chain featuring fashions derived from surfing and snowboarding, sales have leapt from $18 million less than a decade ago to over $320 million in 1998, driven by appeal to teenagers. The Steve Madden shoe line grew 30 percent last year based on its popularity among teenagers. Revenue at Urban Outfitters, noted among teenagers as a neo-grunge chain, jumped 17.5 percent to almost $210 million in 1998.

With this kind of marketplace influence, the already inflated sense of power of Generation Risk is magnified exponentially. This is a generation ready to flex its decision-making muscles. Because they generate so much of their own income, many of today's teenagers are free to determine the way they spend their money.

Yet with this independence comes a new form of pressure. Researchers now know that while part-time work may increase a young person's sense of worth, working too much can be harmful to these kids. Adolescents who work half time or more while attending high school report higher levels of emotional distress, substance abuse, and earlier ages of first sexual intercourse experiences than kids who are concentrating only on school and sports.

In addition, with so many consumer products geared to their tastes, many teens are swept up in the desire for money and what it can buy. Their compulsion to consume is tied to their insatiable hunger for entertainment. Shopping malls have become centers for social activity and hanging out, jammed with visual and audio stimuli as clothing and jewelry stores are clustered with food courts and music outlets. According to the *New York Times*, teenagers average fifty-four shopping trips a year. They are not simply window shopping, either. *Teenage girls alone spend $60 billion a year.*

Based on concern over the influence of media violence on young children and teenagers, parents have traditionally been warned not to use television as a babysitter. But the surrogate babysitter *of this generation* is the shopping mall. For Generation Risk, the lure of the shopping mall is nearly irresistible. It provides an escape from parents and siblings, a chance to talk to friends outside the confines of school, and an opportunity for exposure to *this week's* newest consumables.

Teenagers are in their glory in modern shopping malls with stores targeted directly to their tastes, video arcades placed strategically to attract them, and unsupervised time away from adult influence.

Trisha

Trisha is wearing platform shoes that add about three inches to her height. At fifteen, she is only five feet tall. Trisha's voice is tentative, and her inflection makes almost every comment sound like a question. Trisha loves to hang out at the mall.

"My friend Valerie and me? We went to the mall? And we went into Express? And I was like, 'Oh, Valerie, this is so you! So she got this really cool suede jacket, and she's going to let me wear it, too. We spend our lives at the mall."

The teenagers of Generation Risk are used to being courted by marketers. For example, a new mall is being designed in Orange, California, anchored by a skateboard park and superstore. This showcasing of teenage attractions provides a stark contrast to the full-service department stores that lured shoppers of the past.

Teenagers make their own choices about clothes and personal products, and they do so at increasingly younger ages. Many teenage girls are already using makeup and fragrances by the time they enter middle school. They don't allow their parents to make purchase decisions for them, and instead pick their own brands of hair styling products, cosmetics, deodorants, shaving products, and clothes.

To you as a parent, the financial independence of Generation Risk presents a special challenge. Your authority to regulate what may or may not be purchased is undermined, because *it's not your money* that's being spent. But more diligence than ever is needed to monitor how your teenager is spending his time and money, because there are so many new dangerous options to pursue.

Tattoos and Body Piercings

Tattoos and body piercings are no longer confined to drunken sailors on shore leave. Today's teenagers are just as likely to sport some type of tattoo or piercing, and again, there are no class distinctions in who participates. The irreversible nature of these acts and their visual shock value make them perfect new symbols of independence for risk-seeking teenagers.

Carrie

Carrie's red hair is pulled back into a bun. She is sitting at a table with seven other teenagers in a focus group discussion, leaning forward on her elbows, her head thrust between her hands in a posture of boredom. Her fingers are pushing her checks upward, distorting her face and exaggerating the protrusion of her lips. Carrie is seventeen and wants to be entertained. She would rather be doing almost anything else right now than sitting in this place. She sighs audibly, then listens to the conversation. The group has finally raised a subject that interests her, so she interjects her opinion.

"Tattoos? They're cool. I have a tattoo right here under my shirt. It's a red-headed angel with green eyes, and stars circling all around her head as a halo. She has praying hands, and purple wings that curl up around her with white tips. I picked this tattoo because I think angels are really grace-ful, elegant creatures. I mean, I don't want to look at this thing five years down the road or something and think, 'Oh, my God. How tacky!' It's my thing. If I want you to see it, fine, but if I don't, it's up to me."

The surging popularity of tattoos can be largely attributed to their taboo status. This latest embodiment of audacious self-expression among the under-thirty set is off-limits for most teenagers. The legal age in most places is eighteen for a tattoo or piercing without parental or guardian con-sent. But teenagers have embraced this fad with a passion that says to par-ents, "It's my body. I can do anything with it I want, and you can't stop me."

The leading tattoo magazines are spin-offs of prominent biker publi-cations. From *Easyriders* came *Tattoo* and *Tattoo Flash*, and from *Outlaw Biker* sprang *Tattoo Revue, Tabu Tattoo, Skin Art,* and *Dark Skin Art.* But the tattoo business is hardly contained within the hardcore biker set. The tattoo craze is booming among all segments of society, and it is a perfect medium to convey the gamut of outlandish tastes of the freaky fringe, per-sonal statements by middle-class businesswomen, and expressions of individuality by independent-minded teenagers.

Clinton Sanders, a sociology professor at the University of Connecticut asserts that teenage piercing and tattooing are intended to outrage adults. *Customizing the Body: The Art and Culture of Tattooing* explains the symbolism of this phenomenon, "When a parent freaks out, it's fulfilling its purpose. Teens are showing that they have total control over their bodies."

Ecstasy—A Dangerous New Drug

To add to the already overwhelming array of risks, new substances are continuously being pushed within reach of teenagers. They promise novel and uncharted experiences, and they attract Generation Risk like sugar draws flies.

Of course, once parents become aware that a new drug is gaining popularity among the teen culture, it's probably not really new anymore.

An example is the "love drug" or "hug drug" (*methylenedioximethamphet-amine*, or MDMA), commonly known as "Ecstasy," "Adam," or "X-TC."

Ecstasy is known as a "designer drug" that is popular among young professionals and teenagers from upscale neighborhoods. U.S. Customs officials report than seizures of the drug have nearly tripled from 1997 to 1999 as the drug has quietly crept into the suburban youth culture.

Beliefs about Ecstasy echo misconceptions about LSD in the 1960s, when proponents attributed a range of characteristics to "acid" that later proved false. Today Ecstasy is touted as a route to an altered state of group consciousness, liberation from sexual pressure, and an inspiration for confidence and independence. The drug is sought by teenagers at all-night parties called "raves" to increase trust and break down barriers, mask hunger and fatigue, and produce experience-enhancing hallucinogenic effects.

But researchers also report problems among users of the drug: psychological difficulties including confusion, depression, and paranoia; physical symptoms such as nausea, chills, and involuntary teeth-clenching; and potential permanent damage to the brain.

On a percentage basis, the use of Ecstasy among young people is comparatively small (about 9 percent of women aged fourteen to twenty-four have tried Ecstasy; about 5 percent for men in the same age group.) But there are new dimensions of risk for today's teenagers. On top of their unprecedented accessibility, the popular drugs that entice Generation Risk come with their own Web sites, electronic counterculture support groups, and supercharged mutations. In the case of Ecstasy, a new version called "smacky e's" is laced with heroin to add punch, and another level of danger.

Bidis—A New Fad From India

As if there weren't enough homegrown problems facing America's teenagers, a new fad from India is invading the teenage realm, especially among urban youth. Small, brown hand-rolled cigarettes called bidis (pronounced "beedies") from a variety of southeast Asian countries are growing in popularity among adolescents, and are wrought with dangers.

Bidis are filled with tobacco flakes, hand-rolled with a greenish brown leaf, tapered at both ends, and tied with a tiny, colored thread. The unfiltered cigarettes are shaped like marijuana joints and come in a variety of scents and flavors that hide the harsh taste of the tobacco. They range in cost, but are often sold at about half the price of regular cigarettes.

A recent study in Massachusetts among urban youth (grades 7-12) indicated that 40 percent of kids interviewed had smoked bidis at least once and 16 percent were current bidi smokers. A study in California last year found that over two-thirds of the youths and young adults surveyed knew someone under eighteen who smoked bidis, and that 58 percent of students had tried bidis themselves.

What's particularly frightening about this potent form of cigarette is that bidis are often misunderstood by the kids who smoke them. According to the researchers who published the Massachusetts study, bidis produce three times the amount of carbon monoxide, five times the amount of tar, and three times the amount of nicotine of typical U.S. cigarettes. Yet many of the students in the study said they smoked bidis because they thought they were safer than other cigarettes.

Bidis come in youth-enticing flavors such as bubblegum, strawberry, wild cherry, lemon-lime, and mango. They are about half the size of regular cigarettes and are wrapped in a tendu or temburni leaf (Diospyros melanoxylon), which has low combustibility, so smokers tend to inhale more deeply and more often to keep them lit.

Worse, bidis are frequently produced by low-paid women and child laborers in India, who work under unsanitary conditions, and are totally unregulated by health inspectors.

Naturally, bidis are the new rage among the high school set.

The importance and the menace of fads such as designer drugs or bidis become even more intense when we recognize the influence that peer groups and popular culture exert over our teenagers. In many cases the teenagers of Generation Risk are leading each other toward danger.

PEER PRESSURE AND POPULAR CULTURE: MORE POTENT THAN BEFORE

Unfortunately, adults who spend their days with teenagers do not give glowing reports of teens helping teens. Teachers, coaches, and school administrators say that the peer groups with whom teens are spending so much time are difficult to manage, even in the school environment.

"THESE KIDS ARE OUT OF CONTROL"

Sit in for a moment and listen while a group of middle school and high school teachers and counselors gather in a focus group to talk about the myriad of issues they see and encounter with their students. It is late at night, and they are tired. More than that, they are frustrated and worried about the problems piled on their shoulders.

"These kids are out of control," says Linda, an English teacher in a junior high school. "They're reckless and undisciplined. It must be the combination of sex and drugs and all those hormones raging. I don't know what. But they're aggressive toward adults and toward each other. They slam doors, throw books, turn over chairs. I haven't seen anything like this before in my twenty years of teaching. I don't know what will happen next."

On Linda's right, Paul, a beleaguered-looking high school science teacher, spreads his arms and turns his palms upward in a gesture that seems to invite either sympathy or support. His thinning hair is closely cropped, and his pale blue eyes are watery. He says, "They haven't learned how to control their anger, and they think they don't have to follow the rules. They just don't have anybody to show them how they're supposed to respond. When somebody tells them to do something, it's 100 percent resistance. They're hostile toward it. Just try to tell them not to smoke. They're not going to listen."

A third teacher breaks in to express her frustration in a faltering voice. She is wearing a flowered shirt-waisted dress and sensible flat shoes. She has been teaching at her school for just over three years. "Lack of self-esteem is a huge problem," says Mary Ann. "The students I have, their image is very important to them. But it all centers around risk-taking. It's very frightening. I worry about how these children are going to get through the school year, not even to mention getting an education."

Frank, a large, balding man wearing a frayed brown sweater shifts forward in his chair and sighs deeply. He presses against the sides of his face with both hands in a futile attempt to drive away the onset of a migraine headache.

"I'm supposed to teach these kids algebra and geometry, but I can't even get their attention," he says. " I think maybe we're sending kids the wrong signals about misbehavior. When you put a day care center in the school, you are telling these kids that teen pregnancy is acceptable. It's not okay to smoke. It's not okay to drink. It's not okay just because you're angry to go into a violent rage. But kids see this as normal in the public schools here. We let them think this kind of behavior is acceptable, so why should we expect them to change?"

Linda is intent in her next comment: "We have to make them change. They're headed for disaster. They smoke their cigarettes right out in the open just to show their indifference to us. We supposedly have a smoke-free school, and half of them are in the bathroom lighting up. Or after school, they just step one foot off the school property and stand there puffing away, ignoring what we're telling them. First it's cigarettes, then it's drugs."

A thirty-something track coach, Bob, sits back detached from the group, with his jacket open and his arm draped over the back of the empty chair beside him. When the others finally draw him into the discussion, he sits up straight and counts out the problems on his fingers, one at a time, sizing up the issues like a scout reporting on the competition.

"Look, first of all there's this big national thing about how our kids are smoking. Hey, let me tell you. They're doing a lot more than smoking. Tobacco is the least of the problems. I can't get some of these kids to stay sober enough on a Friday night to be able to run the next day. I've got to worry about drug testing because our whole program could get sanctions. Then at least once a week, I'll have a parent call me and say, 'I can't control my kid anymore. I don't know which way to turn.' Well, they sure as hell can't turn to me. I've got big enough problems of my own with these kids."

Janice is a history teacher in a suburban middle school. She is shocked by the severity of the comments. Janice has been teaching for only two years. "Listen, I think smoking is a big problem. But I don't know how to handle it. And I don't know about all this talk of violence. I mean, I guess there wasn't talk of violence at Columbine either. But my kids are bright, middle-class students, and I wasn't expecting to have any real problems with them. I'm really concerned about the extent of all the smoking and drinking that goes on."

A moderator tries to shift their discussion to the topic of family values.

Eileen has been teaching for twenty years, and has two children of her own. She has a Master's in sociology and teaches a popular class for soph-omores and juniors called "Relationships." "We did a family thing on how to make a friend. 'What is a friend? What are some of your qualifications for a friend?' They had a hard time figuring out what a friend was, and so then we had situations where we said, 'Okay, this is a new student coming into the classroom. How would you begin a conversation?' And you would actually get silence. It truly opened my eyes. I think the simple social skills we take for granted aren't being taught at home anymore."

Mary Ann has been looking at her shoes. She lifts her head, pushes a strand of hair back from her pale face, and ventures an opinion again. She looks a little bit wistful, and slightly sad. "The days of Wally and the Beaver are over. Mother is not there when they come home, fixing them cookies, telling them to drink their milk, and do their homework. Both parents are working, or it's a single parent working."

Eileen jumps in, her voice frenzied and her thoughts running together. She looks worried as she glances from person to person for answers. "We have a lack of trust. These kids lack self-esteem, and related to that is social skills. There's zero ability. Just the simplest things that you used to be able to assume they learned, now they don't know."

Frank shifts sideways in his chair and shakes his head as he looks down at the table in front of him. His shoulders are hunched over in resignation. "I graduated in '72, so what is that—twenty-six years? The way teaching has changed from when I started until now, and the schools, and the students. I think it's unbelievable, and I think for me it gets harder and harder, and more and more demanding, and more and more draining."

The demands on teachers to provide education and maintain basic order in the classroom are too extreme for us to expect them to play the primary role in risk-prevention for our teenagers. They express exasperation, fatigue, and anxiety when faced with the challenges of Generation Risk.

Teenagers Don't Talk to Their Parents about Risks

We hear from teachers that many teenagers are untrusting, untrained in basic social skills, and out of control. But these problems are only part of a larger crisis. Why *else* should parents be concerned? Because of *what we don't know about our teenagers.*

Teenagers build a natural wall around themselves to keep parents off their turf and give them a greater sense of privacy and self-control. Parents bent on enforcing rules miss opportunities to communicate with their kids when problems do arise. Fearing sanctions or other negative repercussions, teenagers would rather go to their peers for advice and counsel. These barriers block parents from helping when teenagers need constructive intervention.

Phyllis

Phyllis is sixteen and has permed blonde hair and a nervous habit of tapping her fingernails on the table. When she talks, she twirls her hair around her index finger. Her boyfriend is eighteen and drives a '95 Camero.

"I go to my sister for advice. She's more my age, and she understands things that go on in school and stuff. People our age live in the kind of world we do. Or I talk to my brother. You can trust your brother or sister. They've done stuff. Stuff that I want to talk to her about, she's done it, too. I've got something on her, so I know she's not going to talk about it. I would not feel comfortable talking to my parents about drugs. No way. You don't want to talk to your parents about everything. I mean, I have safe sex, so there's no problem. But I'd go to my friends before I'd go to my parents. I tend to shut my parents out of my life. Your parents would understand you better really, but you feel closer to your friends. You think you would get into trouble or something."

Teenagers say they often feel more comfortable talking to their friends than to their parents, because friends are not judgmental. Kids seek advice from their peers, most of whom are no more experienced or stable than they are themselves, because peers offer the advantage of neutrality. Even when they don't agree with the behavior of their friends, teenagers rarely confront or criticize each other.

Marina

Marina is fifteen and is wearing carefully applied makeup. Her dark eyes seem to be gazing at a spot on the ceiling, but occasionally flick downward to the interviewer as she talks. She is wearing silver rings on three fingers of her right hand and sports large hoop earrings that sparkle in the light when she casually tosses her head back.

"My mother can't relate to me on any level about drugs or anything. When I try to be open with her and explain to her what goes on, she gets extreme and really like uptight. She so much overreacts. She'll like explode or freak out. So I can't talk to her about it. I don't even try to talk to her."

Because many teenagers won't talk to their parents about issues that are facing them, our close relationships from their early childhood years often fade like distant memories. The longer this isolation from parents persists, the more difficult it becomes to reestablish contact. In the meantime, dangers escalate as teens turn to their friends for guidance.

PEER PRESSURE TO TEENS MEANS PEER ACCEPTANCE

The teenagers of Generation Risk don't think of peer pressure as "pressure" at all. These fun-seeking, self-directed individuals fervently defend their sense of free will when they *decide* to go along with their friends. The glaring irony of this generation is their *conformity to nonconformity*, their keen desire for *individuality* clashing with insecurities and emotional upheavals that make them yearn to belong to a group.

The president of a consulting firm in New York recently quoted one teenager who exemplifies the contradictory logic today's teens apply in making both product and lifestyle choices. The teenager explained that his reason for selecting a particular brand of jeans was that he "wanted to be different, just like everybody else."

Their love affair with risk seems to require this generation of teenagers to be self-sufficient and individual. Teenagers want to make their own decisions, and they feel a strong obligation to allow each other the freedom of choice. They accept risk-taking behavior in their friends because to interfere would be to act like a parent. They don't try to inflict values on each other, and they don't want to be boxed in by the values of their parents. The teenagers of Generation Risk hold sacred their right to make personal choices.

Lavelle

Lavelle is thirteen and feels that people are always telling her what to do. She has large sparkling brown eyes, a bright smile, and a trim figure. She has a new tattoo on her shoulder that says "Lavelle" in dark script letters. Lavelle is looking admiringly at her shoulder thinking that maybe she should add a design under her name. It hasn't occurred to Lavelle that a few years from now she might not want to have a tattoo on her arm. She has heard that tattoos can be removed, and she assumes that it will be just as easy to get rid of a tattoo as it was to get one in the first place.

"Some of my friends think they can do anything, and they don't think of the consequences. But I'm not going to tell them not to do it. They have a right to live their own lives and make their own decisions, just like I do."

Wanting to fit in with each other is a primary motivator for teenagers fighting for individuality and acceptance at the same time. To stand out for the wrong reasons can be the greatest humiliation. They painstakingly observe and imitate the fashion, language, and risky behavior they see in popular culture as they strive to be acknowledged as individuals worthy of belonging.

Yet teenagers make a big point of explaining that the term "*peer pressure*" is misunderstood by adults, and resent the implication that they force each other to take risks or that they are not strong enough or independent enough to make their own choices. Teenagers reject the concept of "peer pressure" because the word "pressure" sounds like coercion.

Ashley

Ashley is wearing layers of clothes, about one layer for each year she has been a teenager. She has selected a short black skirt and a yellow long-sleeved scoop-necked shirt, both with lots of Spandex in the fabric. Over the shirt is a bright red vest. Covering her legs are red-and-yellow-checkered leggings, with black tights peeking out at the ankles. Her jewelry is silver and plentiful, featuring rings, bangle bracelets, and large hoop earrings. Ashley has her own sense of fashion and makes decisions about her clothes based on what she has seen on MTV and in popular magazines.

"Peer pressure is not the way the media makes it sound. Nobody forces you. They don't like say, 'Here, take this.' It's not like that at all. You make your own decisions. I don't know. It's hard to describe peer pressure. I remember people talking about it when we were younger. We got all these D.A.R.E. talks and stuff, and then you actually are there, and it's like not what you think. It's not like people are, 'Come on, come on.' You just want to be like them, you know? I mean, I'm like a junior now, and in high school, I've never been peer pressured to take a puff. You just do it because you want to. It's like people are always curious about things that they can't do, and peer pressure just pushes their wants over the edge."

But despite their protests about individuality and independence, the teenagers of Generation Risk are still dominated by peer influence. They behave like iron filings in a magnetic field, drawn to each other by an unseen force. The homogeneity of their tastes is prominently displayed in their choices of backpacks, music, clothes, and shoes. Their popularization of bands such as the Spice Girls and the Backstreet Boys and their group patronization of teen-targeted chains such as Claire's Stores, Gadzooks, and Hot Topic are evidence of the power of what's "in" and their need to be part of it.

Most teenagers acknowledge that the behavior of their friends is a big influence on what they choose to do. If their friends smoke, they will probably try it, too. They attribute the striking conformity of their behavior to a general curiosity about the things their friends are doing, and a desire to fit in. Researchers believe that much of the risk-taking normally attributed to peer pressure is really an attempt by teenagers to initiate new relationships or group memberships, to promote cohesion, trust, and closeness among friends.

Jeff

Jeff's hair is parted in the middle and is supposed to be combed toward the sides, but springs back whenever he pushes it down. He has a two-tiered haircut, long on top and shaved on the lower level. Jeff's complexion is a problem for him. His face is dotted with red marks from acne, and he's wondering whether it will ever clear up.

"Peer pressure is kind of a crock. It's not like where everybody surrounds you and forces you to smoke a joint. It's like, 'Do you want to do this?' If it's 'no' they'll leave you alone. It's not like they pressure you into it. Like, some of my friends dropped out of school, but I'm still in school. People that give in to peer pressure have mixed emotions. You really don't know. Then you think, 'I wonder what that would be like.' If you're weak, you're going to do it. But mostly you just want to be with your friends."

Most of these teenagers would far rather hang out with friends than spend time with their families. The contrast between the high-impact stimulation of much of their lives versus the relative calm of their home environments creates a vacuum for the members of Generation Risk just waiting to be filled with some form of excitement. Teenagers want to be sociable and spend time with their friends doing anything that seems like fun—but, most importantly, to keep from being *bored,* a condition they describe as a nearly intolerable state of vegetation.

This socialization process is normal for adolescents, and parents want their teenagers to have friends and to have fun. "Hanging out with friends" sounds innocent enough, just a way to pass the time after school and before enforced homework hours. But it is vital for parents to understand that when family support is lacking, teenagers are more easily influenced by peers and more likely to seek peer approval through extreme behaviors.

Andy

Andy is a freshman in high school who likes to hang out with his friends. Most of the time they don't have anything too exciting to do, so they watch television or go to a movie. Sometimes they go out for a pizza, or to a football game, or just drive around. Andy has a part-time job a couple of nights a week, and he earns enough spending money to suit himself. His parents pay for his clothes. Andy is wearing a pair of khaki shorts, a hooded Abercrombie sweatshirt (a "hoodie"), and Birkenstock sandals. His T-shirt sticks out about three inches below the bottom of his sweatshirt.

"I don't really want to spend time at home. I want to be with my friends. It's nice because you can just have fun doing whatever you feel like doing. I like to play ball, hang out, just go around to friends' houses and goof off. I mean, I like just jumping in the car, just driving around, causing chaos. Flirting with the girls. Sitting around, chilling. You get together with your friends, and you just get in the car and go blow your paycheck, basically. On anything that sounds good. Just go out and blow it. [Andy laughs.] Then you wish you hadn't."

Warning teenagers of Generation Risk about the dangers of peer pressure doesn't work. As a parent, if you characterize peer pressure as a *bad thing,* you miss the point. To teenagers of this generation, peer influence is a *good thing.* They *want to be invited* to be part of the group. However, you can help your teenager learn how to judge when the group is going astray. Your teenager needs tools and techniques to be prepared to embrace the highly prized feeling of belonging but, at the same time, to direct peer interaction toward positive activities. You can be instrumental in building these skills in your teenager, but first it's helpful to consider the culture in which these peer groups function. They are linked inextricably.

THEY'RE PLUGGED INTO POPULAR CULTURE

Popular culture reflects the attitudes and activities of modern society and is especially important to the teenagers of Generation Risk, who no longer depend on their parents for information or advice. The tutors of this generation are digitized images from television, movies, computers, and music videos that feed them ideas about fashion, language, and social acceptability.

Popular culture can be all-consuming for teenagers surrounded by electronic stimuli and mass media. Current styles, successful brands, box-office stars, fads, and trends are established through sitcoms, the Internet, and movies and reinforced through magazines, newspapers, and teen-directed advertising. The tentacles of popular culture reach out and wrap themselves around teenagers like the appendages of a giant squid.

This is a generation fed by visual imagery. Children in America devote more time to watching television than to any other waking activity. Television and movies, as the windows to popular culture, have a tremendous impact on teenagers, influencing attitudes about sexuality, fashion, and brands, and promoting multidimensional forms of risk-taking.

MTV is the network of Generation Risk. The elements of popular culture and advertising that drive this generation are high-tech images of independence, exhilaration, and adventure. Movies that command large crowd appeal often have violent, destructive themes, and heroes are often portrayed as smokers, drinkers, sexually liberated, risk-takers—or all of the above.

But what's *new* about the influence of popular culture on Generation Risk? Its *power*. The impact of popular culture is magnified by the accessibility of images and messages through electronic media. In the midst of this technological revolution, your parental role as a teacher and provider of information has been usurped by digital imagery. There are no surprises for this savvy new generation: they've already seen it all on Ricki Lake.

As a parent, it's important that you acknowledge that times have changed and recognize that today's teenagers have been exposed to much more, much earlier than generations of the past. Teenagers can easily become disenfranchised from parents who fail to appreciate the accelerated pace of teenage living in the new millennium—just at a critical time when parental influence is vitally important. While teenagers may feel independent and self-sufficient in this modern age, their need for your positive influence and your advice about values has not diminished. More than ever, the teenagers of Generation Risk need stability, role models, counsel, and structure to guide them through the thicket of influences that comprise popular culture.

Cigarettes as a Badge of Popular Culture

The stars of modern movies set poor examples for Generation Risk. Julia Roberts' background as a prostitute in *Pretty Woman* is mildly dismissed by its fairy tale ending. Nicolas Cage smokes his way through the seamy world of porn movies and sexual exploitation in *8mm*. Advertisements for *Fear and Loathing in Las Vegas* show a distorted, morphing version of Johnny Depp looking drugged-out and weird, oversized sunglasses reflecting the bright neon lights, with a cigarette holder clamped in his teeth.

The blockbuster success of *Titanic*, which grossed $580 million in the U.S., was largely accounted for by teenage girls, who contributed an estimated 30 to 40 percent of the take. Heartthrob Leonardo DiCaprio not only smokes throughout the movie, but rolls his own.

Smoking is an integral part of popular culture, and teenagers see it as a pervasive activity in a world rife with personal indulgences and excesses. Many of the heroes and role models of this generation represent extremes. Television, movies, and youth-oriented magazines celebrate peer group identification and rejection of moderation.

The values and interests of teenagers are largely dictated by what they see and hear, and most of the content of pop culture is not especially cerebral. Teenagers appear far less concerned about government and history than rock music and television. According to a survey by the National Constitution Center, 81 percent of American youth recognize the rock group Hanson, but only 21 percent know how many legislators there are in the U.S. Senate. There are similar awareness gaps for events of historical importance versus television icons. Only 25 percent know where the Constitution was written (Philadelphia), but 75 percent can identify "*90210*" as a California ZIP code because of the trendy television show by that name.

Because teenagers often emulate the role models they see on television and in movies, parents must react to this social milieu in a different way from parents of the past. The more you exaggerate the dangers of cigarette smoking to this generation, the more attractive it becomes. This generation is reaching for ways to be stimulated. Danger is not a word of warning to Generation Risk; it is an invitation. The *No Fear* brand of clothing is the hallmark of this generation.

Popular Culture and Sports Heroes

Body art and other reflections of popular culture are showcased by another set of heroes of Generation Risk: professional athletes. There is no better pictorial essay of popular culture than televised sports, depicting the fervor of competitors and spectators alike and the battle for control and order by officials. Sporting events themselves evoke a brand of excitement based on extreme behavior. Football players celebrate particularly physical tackles. Penalties for unnecessary roughness, roughing the passer, roughing the kicker, and personal fouls abound. Taunting and faceoffs between players punctuate the official competitive action.

In a similar way, basketball has evolved into a *contact sport* with nearly every shot or move to the basket inviting a potential foul call. Athleticism is paired with physical strength and aggressive play to define stardom. As positive as Michael Jordon has been as a role model for youth, the bad-boy image of Dennis Rodman competes for teenage loyalty on the court and in advertising media.

Pro wrestling is now the darling of Generation Risk; its icons are emblazoned on clothing and bouts are featured on cable television. Hockey is becoming another adored sport of this generation, founded on fast-paced action and violence, with fans and participants screaming for body contact.

This sphere of popular culture communicates that stronger is better and power wins ball games. The implication to teenagers of Generation Risk is that aggressive behavior leads to success. Tough guys win. The message many kids take away is that they should be able to handle any risk—smoking, drinking, whatever. The clear deduction for parents is that more powerful parental intervention is needed to counterbalance the effects of popular culture with family values.

EARLY INDEPENDENCE MAKES TEENAGERS PARTICULARLY VULNERABLE

Social scientists have concluded that teenagers today are different from any previous generation because they have grown up more independently. Researchers assert that today's teenagers are more self-reliant because they come from single-parent families or two-parents-working households, and have been making their own decisions for years. But while early independence may boost self-confidence in some ways, teenagers on their own are increasingly open to outside influences.

The forces of peer pressure and popular culture are powerful and omnipresent. Like marketers challenged to break through the clutter to reach consumers with their messages, parents must find ways of appealing to these teenagers that transcend the seductive forces of modern society.

If you want to reach your teenager in the age of Generation Risk, you have to begin by acknowledging the formidable influences of peer groups and popular culture. Your opportunity to influence your teenager depends on building a solid foundation *in the context of these factors.*

The teenagers of Generation Risk are barreling head-on through their lives without regard for contingency plans. Reaching out to teenagers of this generation without the right preparation is like battling a raging fire without training or equipment.

As a parent, your first task is to establish a foundation of credibility and sensitivity. Until teenagers have confidence that parents understand and care about their feelings, they will never accept our advice.

Prevention researchers understand the "risk factors and protective factors" that weight the odds of teenage involvement in smoking, alcohol and drug abuse, unprotected sex, pregnancy, and violence. Psychologists offer programs based on social learning theory to build "life skills" that help adolescents cope with stress and change. Teenagers who are strongly connected to their families are more likely to resist the influences of peer groups and popular culture and less likely to smoke and take other risks.

In the following section of the book, we'll discuss ways to reconnect with your teenager to build a healthy foundation for your relationship—the cornerstone to being able to guide your teen on the often perilous pathway of growing up.

PART II

LAYING THE FOUNDATION

5

CONNECTEDNESS: A POWERFUL PROTECTIVE FACTOR FOR YOUR TEEN

As a parent, you may think you know your teenager because you have spent so many years together as part of the same family. But in this fast-paced age, all you have to do is look away briefly and everything changes.

Like ducklings transforming themselves into adult birds, teenagers have traditionally changed in predictable ways, losing the baby down that marked them so distinctively as belonging to childhood. As they reached maturity, they slowly developed a new look and identity.

The transformation still occurs, but the teenagers of Generation Risk are morphing at high speed, accelerated by a more extreme form of external stimuli than their predecessors encountered, including video arcades, rap music, easy access to material goods, and unsupervised exposure to potent and destructive substances and activities.

75

Because the pace of our world is so fast and the external forces are so far beyond what most parents would find appropriate for their children, studies are showing that our kids need more than ever for us to be a part of their lives.

An Adolescent Health Study on youth behavior, published in 1997, confirmed the importance of strong relationships among teenagers, families, and schools. The study evaluated the ways in which adolescents connect to their social world, and the influence of these social settings and connections on health. What is very evident from this research is that your child benefits from strong *connections* to family and school.

If there is a high degree of "connectedness"—closeness, caring, and satisfaction—within the family, teenagers are less likely to think about or attempt suicide; and less likely to use cigarettes, alcohol, and marijuana. This relationship extends to the school. If teens feel noticed, respected, and wanted—connected—to the school, they are more likely to feel close to people at school. This form of connectedness also reduces levels of emotional distress among teenagers; protects them from cigarette, alcohol, and marijuana use; and makes them more likely to delay their first experience in sexual intercourse until an older age.

To complete this equation, when parents have high expectations for their teenagers' academic success and respect and value the school, teenagers report lower levels of emotional distress and are less likely to smoke cigarettes or engage in violent behavior. But it doesn't work for parents just to have high expectations without involvement as well.

The conclusions from this research are critically important to the parents of Generation Risk. Connections with teenagers are fragile, like threads that unravel under pressure. Relationships with Generation Risk teenagers are especially vulnerable to breaking down during the years when these teens are seeking independence and individuality. Children may enter adolescence as well behaved, compliant, and conforming, but as teenagers they are likely to become rebellious, contentious, and independent.

To play a key role in helping your teenager through this tumultuous stage, you should purposely plan activities that involve her with the entire family. You have to demonstrate that you recognize the new levels of maturity your teenager is reaching.

Talk to her about what's happening in her life, find out more about what she thinks, and get involved in her school. Your role can be as simple as supporting the team at "home" games or as structured as taking on a job with the PTA. Most schools also have ways to use volunteers on an occasional basis. Any officer of the PTA would be happy to talk with you about the possibilities. By becoming active with the school, you'll get to know other parents as well as staff members, and your actions will show your teenager that you think her world is important.

The more you understand about what is taking place in her life (and in her mind when she'll tell you), the better chance you have to help her. Prying or pushing into her world won't work, but being available usually will. She's the same six-year-old who couldn't wait for you to arrive to see the kindergarten class play. She still cares very much what you think; she's just gotten good at hiding it.

But to better manage your efforts to establish a connection with your teenager, it's important to understand some of what parents do that inadvertently causes a "disconnect" with their teens.

THE IMPORTANCE OF HONESTY: "THERE'S NO SANTA CLAUS, AND WHAT ELSE?"

As little children grow from infancy to early childhood, they learn thousands of facts, skills, and rules. Adults set boundaries to protect children from danger and supply them with guidance to help them grow and develop. Parents also perpetuate magical myths such as Santa Claus and the Tooth Fairy because these fantasies provide children with excitement, anticipation, and incentives to behave. *"He knows when you've been sleeping; He knows when you're awake; He knows when you've been bad or good; So be good for goodness sake."*

In their early years, children are taught that certain things are wonderful and other things are dangerous. They believe these lessons. They learn to look both ways before crossing the street. They know never to touch any bottle marked POISON and not to play with fire. They heed warnings not to take candy from strangers.

In primary and elementary schools, children are exposed to a whole variety of new facts and new warnings. First-and second-graders are told that drugs are dangerous, that drinking liquor could turn them into alcoholics, and that cigarettes cause diseases. Little kids often come home from school and admonish their parents for having a beer or smoking a cigarette, or even beg their parents to stop these behaviors. We never hear about little children who say they intend to become drinkers or smokers or drug users later in their lives.

Then something happens, about the time they move from the relatively warm and cuddly years of early childhood to the confusing, conflicting, and confounding years of adolescence. Teenagers are exposed to new truths. They realize that if they twist their faces into distorted shapes, their features will not really "freeze" as they were overwarned by well-intentioned parents. Like Cinderella's magical spell that was broken at midnight, the fantasies children have believed in are shattered and replaced with stark reality when they become teenagers. They grow distrustful of authority. They question the accuracy of some of the warnings they had wholeheartedly accepted earlier.

Marvin

Marvin is wearing his Yankee's baseball cap turned around at an angle so that the opening at the back of the cap hits his forehead just above the right eyebrow. He always wears his cap this way. It's his signature style. Marvin is a high school senior with opinions to express. His large frame fills the chair, and his presence fills the room as he leans forward and begins to speak.

"A long time ago my grandmother told me coffee stunts your growth. My health teacher said it's not true. When I heard that, I felt mad. My grandmother, she lied to me. When I asked her, she said she just told me that 'cause she didn't want me to drink it. She said I'd jump off the walls. Well, I don't know if I can trust my grandmother now. I don't want people to lie to me."

Teenagers of Generation Risk interpret deception as a lack of respect, the ultimate insult. They are used to respect and even deference from retailers, moviemakers, and Internet marketers. They expect as much from parents.

Parents don't reach this point intending to be deceptive. They build up the magic of Santa and other childhood myths for a whole range of positive reasons: to fill children with excitement, to titillate them with anticipation, and to inspire them with wonder. Many parents have made extreme categorical statements about the dangers of certain activities, again for positive reasons: to fence children off from perils, to make children aware of their surroundings, and to build resistance.

But in the age of Generation Risk, there are no protective wrappings for children. Well before they are fully mature, these kids have been exposed to the realities of life as depicted by Hollywood, cable television and television talk shows. Teenagers think they know how to handle adult life just because they've seen it portrayed on their video screens.

To be an effective parent to this savvy and information-rich generation, you have to build credibility. You have to supplement protective instincts with honest communication or else your teenager will discount your advice as being irrelevant, exaggerated, and out of touch. If you deceive your children through exaggeration, they will resent it. The following example of Volare is an extreme reaction to the more-or-less harmless childhood myth of Santa Claus, but imagine how Volare and others like her feel when parents don't get their facts straight or don't tell the truth about important issues including smoking, drinking, drugs, or teen health issues such as eating disorders.

Volare

Volare is sitting at the table drinking a Diet Coke from a can. She is wearing a dark green nylon warm-up jacket with a broad purple stripe that runs from the shoulders all the way down the sleeves. Her curly brown hair is parted on the right side and hangs at her shoulders, spilling forward to cover most of her wide, round face. She is carrying a black backpack and wearing blue and white Adidas running shoes and faded blue jeans with a rip at the right knee. Her jacket covers most of her body. Volare is fifteen, and is worried about being fat. She has been peeking at the latest issue of *Teen People* featuring an article about Leonardo DiCaprio.

"I yelled at my mom for fooling me that there was a Santa Claus. I was mad, seriously angry with her for lying to me. Most kids are like, 'Whatever,' when they find out about Santa Claus. But if someone lies to me, I don't want to trust them again. It really bothered me that my mother lied to me."

To some kids, truth is an absolute, and their trust is fragile. To fool this generation, to beguile them, or even to entertain them with well-meaning falsehoods undermines their trust. You can't expect to keep secrets from this generation.

Kelsee

Kelsee is a high school sophomore with two older sisters and two younger brothers. She is determined to make the cheerleading team. Her blond hair is long and full, and it bounces when she nods her head. Kelsee ends most of her comments with a nod. She is wearing an orange halter top and white shorts that show off her athletic figure. Her earrings are miniature pom-poms in orange and white, the school colors set in constant motion.

"My parents told me, 'Watching TV too close will make you blind.' Or they say, 'Don't make a funny face, or it will stay that way.' But it makes you feel stupid when you hear something like that. You feel confused when you find out later that it's not true. You're starting to wonder how come they told you that. I mean, even small things are lies. A lie is still a lie. You can't tell children just everything. There are some things a child can't handle. But you have to treat them with respect, not just like something you own. I don't want to confuse my children. Small things are important."

WITH LACK OF TRUST, KIDS TAKE SERIOUS TRUTHS TO BE AGE-OLD MYTHS

For teenagers accustomed to unmasking parental myths, the dangers of smoking, drinking, or drug use can easily fall into this category of abandoned beliefs. Generation Risk has been warned about the consequences of these behaviors. But what do they see? Teenagers see their peers participating in risky behaviors. But generally what they see is tolerance. They see kids taking a drink or becoming drunk, then recovering. They see kids smoking cigarettes, but not contracting lung cancer. Many teenagers believe they can handle these activities and that the consequences were exaggerated by the adults who warned them not to touch.

The occasional tragic consequences of drug overdoses, alcohol poisoning, or drunken driving are aberrations that are mourned and then discounted by Generation Risk.

If your child has been through the D.A.R.E. program (Drug Abuse Resistance Education program that has been used nationally throughout our school systems), you may feel that much of your work has been done for you. Unfortunately, many researchers now believe that the program suffers from the credibility problem we've been discussing. Young children respond positively when police officers come to their schools and talk to them about the hazards of cigarettes, alcohol, and drugs. But the D.A.R.E. program loses momentum and effectiveness when these same kids progress to higher grade levels and face the tidal wave of challenges and temptations that awaits them. While the D.A.R.E. program increases knowledge and social skills, it does not effectively modify use of substances. Regardless of how deeply they believe the police officer when they are ten or eleven, kids grow up to see parents drinking, older siblings smoking, and friends urging them to give one of these substances a try.

As children are catapulted into their teenage years, disillusioned about many of their early childhood beliefs, they are still ill-prepared to handle the barrage of pressures that will face them. Their changing bodies and coursing hormones urge them to experiment with previously forbidden goods. Their systems of beliefs are changing too. No longer are the adults in their lives the most important influences. The age of the peer group has arrived.

Most kids have been warned about peer pressure and have been cautioned not to "go along with the crowd." But rarely have kids really been prepared to deal with the new demands and temptations of their teenage years. They have not been taught about assertiveness or refusal skills. Their defenses are down, and their desires to fit in with their friends are at an all-time high. They need someone to trust.

But these are the times when adults often lose contact with their teenagers, because value systems are changing so radically, communication is eroding, and the consequences of being completely open with parents may not be worth the effort.

Baron

Baron is seventeen. His short hair is curly and dark, pushed back from his forehead and standing up on top of his head like a deep pile carpet. His sideburns are shaped into wedges that extend straight down along his ear and spike forward toward his nose. The braces on his teeth reflect in the light as he flashes a grin.

"My Dad said, 'If you want to drink, just drink at our house.' I knew that was just an invitation to get a beating. I think that because a lot of parents are hard on their kids or tell them not to do this and that, we lie and keep things secret. We're afraid of the reaction our parents will have if they find out what we're doing."

THE HARM IN OVERPROTECTION

The temptation to overprotect teenagers may be stronger than ever before among the parents of Generation Risk. With all the obvious signs of danger, the most natural parental instincts are to forbid, to restrict, and to deny teenagers in an effort to protect them from harm.

Volare

Volare has postponed reading her article about Leonardo DiCaprio. She is tucking it into her backpack to read again later. She has pictures of Leonardo pasted on the wall above her bed and plans to add this one to the collection as soon as she gets home.

"My mom has this 'automatic no' issue whenever I ask her permission to do anything. You would just ask about something, or tell her about something that happened, and then she'd get mad and be like, 'Okay, you're grounded.' Your parents always freak out. They always overexaggerate."

Volare's mother is attempting to protect her from places and situations where she feels her teenager will be at risk. But by responding with what Volare describes as an "automatic no," she is denying her daughter the opportunity to experience new things and to learn how to handle herself in various circumstances.

But no parent should respond with an "automatic yes" to give a teen experience, either. You should take time to hear your child out, asking about safety precautions that may already be in place. In this way you can begin to help your teenager build strength of character for making some of his own decisions about when the answer should be "yes" and when it should be "no." If you've always said the "no" for him, he'll have had no opportunity to try saying it for himself.

This process is not easy on parents. For example, when our daughter Natalie was learning to drive, we spent many hours together learning to shift gears, practicing turns, parallel parking, and generally working on safe driving techniques. At the time, I thought the sound of the gears grinding and the snapping sensation in my neck as we lurched forward would be the worst aspects of the experience, but they were only minor compared to the knot I felt in my stomach the first time she took the car out on her own on the highway. Suddenly the consequences of "letting her make her own mistakes" became life-threatening. Though I knew she was as well-prepared as I could make her to be a good and safe driver, the act of letting her go off on her own was really tough.

In the same way, we have to give our kids the latitude to make their own decisions on many levels. We can help instill skills, principles, and rules, but we can't always be there in the passenger seat giving advice and warnings. Our teenagers have to grow up and take control of their own lives.

RELATING TO PARENTS

Today's teenagers clearly belong to a new generation, distinct and separate from their parents. Most of them agree that adults who can relate to them are rare specimens. Part of the problem for Generation Risk comes from having so much unstructured time on their hands. Teens who spend less time with parents spend more time with peers, and are therefore more vulnerable to peer influence.

Laura

Laura has only three more weeks of high school. She is sick of studying and doesn't much see the point in doing her homework for the rest of the year. She's a senior, and she thinks she deserves a little "slack." Laura knows she wants to be a hairdresser because her aunt does hair and has taught her all about it. She thinks she can earn more than enough to share an apartment with two of her friends and be on her own—and then her mother won't bother her about smoking and staying out late and every other thing on earth.

"My mother, she thinks everything is still old like she is. She's the old school. She tries to make you act like the way she did. 'No parties without chaperones.' That's so out of it. Or, 'When you go out with a boy, he should come to the house to pick you up.' We're in the new millennium. We do things our own way. We want to try stuff out. There's always parties going on. There's always drinking. There's always drugs. Sex and drugs, alcohol and drugs. It's like a big thing at parties. My mother always says, 'I never did that when I was your age.' She doesn't relate to me."

Teenagers who see their friends relating to parents are often baffled and envious. They simply can't picture relating so closely with their own parents, because they have not seen a demonstration of understanding by their parents.

Valerie

Valerie is fourteen years old. She has just finished lunch at Taco Bell with her friend Leslie. After the interview, they will spend the afternoon at the mall—shopping, hanging out, and listening to the new CDs at the music store. Valerie is worried that she might be pregnant.

"One of my friends at school is really, like, close with her mom. She can talk to her about everything, like boys and smoking and stuff like that. Her mom just has one of those personalities that you can really open up to. But like with my mom, I can never see myself talking about the stuff that my friend is talking to her mom about. It's like my mom always thinks, 'I'm the parent. I just know what is best for you, so just listen to me.' Even though she may be right, sometimes you just want her to talk to you as an equal instead of always

being the child. Or if you ask a question, she won't give you an answer. It's like you're in a monopoly, like she's the queen and you're the servant."

An important ingredient in the recipe for relating to teenagers is to treat them with respect. These teenagers resent one-sided relationships with parents. Teenagers can appreciate the protective instincts of their parents, but feel unnecessarily sheltered. Many see parents as one-dimensional and even naïve in their roles as protectors.

Susan

Susan wants to be a nutritionist. Her father is a dentist and she thought about being a dentist, but she doesn't really like other people's teeth. What Susan likes is to give other people advice. Susan is wearing black capri pants and a red scooped-neck shirt with three-quarter–length sleeves. Her shoes are black leather sandals, open at the back and toe, with a small heel because she is so tall. She is thinking about lunch and trying to decide what to eat and what to advise her friend Laura to eat.

"I find that my parents are so far from experiencing things, like it's been decades, that they're like totally concerned about protecting me and they're not as concerned about relating. They're just kind of, 'We want to protect you.' I think they're protective because things have changed. There weren't as many drugs when they were my age. I'll be eighteen in July, and my parents still try that trip about sex. And I'm like, 'Did you not think I was going to like guys?' I'm not five."

The teenagers of Generation Risk know that parents do not approve of the reckless and dangerous behaviors that are standard among today's teenagers. But to inform parents is asking for confrontation and disapproval, so most teenagers reluctantly keep many of their concerns and activities hidden from parents.

Michelle

Michelle is from Florida. She has blonde, shoulder-length permed hair, but she blow-dries it straight because she doesn't like the perm. She always puts butterfly clips or sequined sparkles or something in her hair to dress it up. She never just wears her hair down. Today she is using her sunglasses to push her hair back from her face, even though it is already dark outside. The frames of her sunglasses are lavender. The lenses are black. Michelle is fourteen.

"Most parents aren't aware of what's going on with, like, the smoking and your friends. Your parents have to tell you what's right and wrong. That's their job. So you don't want to talk about the things which you know they're going to say are wrong. Parents have to not get mad at you when you tell them something. Sometimes teenagers go to their friends' parents instead of their own, because they don't get grounded by their friends' parents. Your parents can give you a lot of good advice by just talking about anything. I have asked my mom's advice. Sometimes I just think about how hard school is, and things stress me out. I think if I talked to my parents they could help me out. You want to feel like there's somebody there when you want to talk."

The teenagers of Generation Risk are used to taking chances. With their constant exposure to electronic media and open access to information, many of them feel that they don't need to rely on parents to educate them. Combined with normal adolescent feelings of insecurity, this insular attitude causes many teenagers to avoid talking to parents at all. They have to be invited.

Cindy

Cindy is putting on her makeup. She is just finishing the hint of eyeliner and a trace of blusher, then just a dab of mascara and some lip gloss. She rushed out of the house without finishing her eye makeup because her mother was getting on her nerves, and she just had to get away. Cindy is thirteen, and seems to fight with her mother most of the time. She is closer to her father, but doesn't really spend much time with either of them. She'd rather be over at a friend's house.

"If I can't trust my parents with something, I won't go to them. They have to show interest. If they're sarcastic or something, you don't want to talk to them. So they have to make you feel like they care more about what you're saying than about how smart they're gonna look giving you a brilliant response."

It Takes Time To Connect

One of the keys to developing skills in teenagers is to spend time with them in ways you both enjoy, to get them involved in activities that build up their physical abilities, social skills, and self-esteem. To appreciate the perspective of your teenager, you have to share some of the same experiences. You have to discuss your opinions about things you both see and hear. You have to invest time in consciously seeking to understand what makes your teenager angry, what gets him excited, what he loves, and what he rejects.

In a startling work called *Being Adolescent,* Mihaly Csikzentmihalyi and Reed Larson reported that adolescents spend less than 5 percent of their time with their parents and only an additional 2 percent of their time with other adults. With such limited time together, parents must focus on *effective* interaction.

Baron

Baron is drumming his fingers on the table and hopping his right leg up and down. He has been wanting to talk to his father about getting a new video game, but isn't sure how to bring up the topic. Baron is bored most afternoons after school, but all his father ever talks to him about is grades and studying—like that's what he should do all day after school. Homework is so dull. His father just doesn't understand.

"I think it really helps to get involved with your kids. Some of my friends have been in soccer since they've been three years old and basketball and all these sports and the fun things, and the parents go to all the games, or maybe even coach a town team. My family never was into that. Parents should do fun things with their kids and not just the bad stuff like cleaning and stuff. Just do some things that are fun."

Part of the challenge of becoming involved with your teen is remembering that just because you were a great guard on your school's basketball team, that may not be what interests him or what he is good at. You've got to see your child as an individual and recognize that he is separate and distinct from you.

IT'S NOT ABOUT YOU

Renowned psychologist Erik Erikson, who developed the concept of "identity formation," believed that adolescence is a period when young people shape a focused, personal identity by searching for models, roles, and values. In order to establish independent identities, teenagers often rebel against parental authority.

Rebellion among teenagers takes on many forms. Their ways of expressing themselves may be different, but teenagers are all going through major transitions and must find ways of separating themselves from parental control. In many cases, that also means separating themselves from parental approval.

Parents must be careful to look for subtle problems, not just the obvious ones, and avoid becoming complacent just because teenagers may seem to be on the right track. Temptations, conflicts, threats, and pressures can arise at any time, not just during the early teenage years. Here's an example that applies.

My darling daughter Natalie has been a real joy to my husband and me in many ways. She is beautiful, smart, athletic, and self-confident. She has always been well-organized, even when she was a toddler. She used to sit on the kitchen floor in her jammies-with-the-feet-in while I cooked dinner, and stack and restack her jars of baby food in the lower kitchen cabinet.

She is a college student now, and feels pretty independent and self-sufficient. Natalie has her life in good order. She has a career goal in mind, plans to attend graduate school, and has already lined up her job for the coming summer. I have felt really proud of Natalie and have trusted her judgment for a long time.

Recently, she tentatively raised a subject with those words that make parents cringe at the end of the telephone line, "*Mom, I want to tell you about something that you're not going to like.*" She then proceeded to explain that she had thought about it for a long time, researched the idea, delayed, considered, and finally decided—to have her tongue pierced! I was stunned and disgusted by this announcement. I couldn't understand why a seemingly level-headed, intelligent young girl would even consider such a grotesque idea.

She further explained that she had already had this abomination completed about two weeks earlier. She reassured me there was no longer a chance of infection, that she was carefully following directions about caring for the "wound," and that "you can't even see it unless I open my mouth." Next came the "logic," explaining that at least it wasn't a tattoo that everybody could see all the time, and that she probably wouldn't even have this tongue ring (or whatever it's called) when she was thirty!

When I reacted negatively (this is an understatement), Natalie kept trying to point out that her actions had nothing to do with her father or me—that it was just about her, not about us. Well, we didn't see it that way.

I thought we had made it through safely with Natalie. She is past her most vulnerable teenage years. But apparently some lingering vestiges of rebellion took hold of her. Her insistence that her actions had nothing to do with parental relationships simply didn't seem accurate to me. She had certainly provoked a parental reaction. Secondly, I wasn't doing a good job of dealing with the news. I was upset, preoccupied, and bewildered. I turned to my friends for help.

I asked for my sister's advice, and my mother's advice. I asked my friends at work to help me think of a way to convince Natalie to get rid of the tongue ring—immediately. Oddly, nobody was able to help. The advice I got from all directions was practically the same: "Get over it," or "Don't sweat the little things." I couldn't understand how so many normally sensible people could be so wrong about this issue.

Then my best friend reminded me that just a year or two before, I had encouraged her to think about all the positive things about her teenage son when he was behaving like a stereotypical teenager and driving her to distraction. "Remember what you told me," she said. "Natalie's still a wonderful person, and you should look at all the positive things. You should think about all the other things she might have done but didn't."

I have now reluctantly adjusted to the idea of Natalie's tongue being her own, but I still don't want to look at it. The point of this story is that we can never stop being parents and wanting to make decisions for our children, especially when we think they are making bad ones. Yet the older they get, the more right they think they have to make their own decisions.

Even more importantly, as my daughter tried to explain to me, this decision had nothing to do with me as a parent. It was an expression of independence by my daughter that had everything to do with *her*.

Recognizing the teenagers of Generation Risk as independent entities is a vital step for parents. To communicate effectively, you have to acknowledge that your teenager is autonomous and *not just an extension of you*. You have to provide enough latitude for your teenager to act differently than you would act in some situations, and then be willing to listen to and accept her reasons why.

BIG BROTHERS, BIG SISTERS, AND BIG IDEAS

Big Brothers Big Sisters, a nonprofit organization dedicated to helping troubled kids through their childhood and teen years, has developed a model from which we can learn. Their program is based on mentoring and empowerment, and the goal is to build attachments between people, much like the bonds between parents and their children. It measures its results in terms of risks avoided: less involvement in alcohol, drugs, violence, teen pregnancy, smoking, and other negative behaviors. According to Fred Rickman, who heads the organization in southwest Louisiana, perhaps the most important skill adults can display is good listening: "Adults can provide children with a sense of self-worth based on knowing that someone cares enough to spend time with them, to be there with them, to listen to them.", he says. "If children feel that everything they say is important, then they feel a sense of real importance, of being loved and valued. All kids are all hungry for that."

For mentors (or parents), Big Brothers Big Sisters believes that satisfying your own needs first is part of being effective. Then you will be better prepared to transfer positive feelings to your children, and you will have more credibility with them when you give advice. Your teenager has to believe your advice is worth following. Rickman explains that if you don't govern your own life successfully, your teenager will be unlikely to trust you to manage his. "If kids don't see us as happy, fulfilled individuals, we are pretty powerless to have much of an impact on their values and their thoughts," he says, "They look at our lifestyle and say, 'Well, you know, that doesn't seem to be working, so why should I try to emulate it?' I think they have a good point."

Another important ingredient in the Big Brothers Big Sisters recipe is empowerment. One of the ways to build self-esteem among kids is to trust them to make certain decisions, even if they make some mistakes. What's central is to believe in their ability to make decisions on their own and to give them a chance to come up with some of their own solutions, a responsibility they'll inevitably be faced with later.

Perhaps the most powerful part of the Big Brothers Big Sisters model involves acceptance, which tends to be easier for siblings than it is for parents. Our instincts as parents are to try to correct problems immediately, but brothers or sisters are much more tolerant.

There's a reason why this organization is called Big Brothers Big Sisters. The closeness teenagers feel for their siblings is based on a certain degree of equality, on tolerance and understanding, and on freedom to act. Brothers and sisters care about each other, but they tend to be less judgmental and restrictive than parents. They give each other credit for having reached whatever level of maturity they have attained. Mr. Rickman suggests being more accepting of teenagers and helping them work through their own issues through a combination of listening and caring instead of judging and pushing: "Just try to understand where the kid is coming from on the issues that bother you, and keep on loving them," he says, "It's better to allow them to reach a more mature level, to let them get to the point where they want to do something about their own issues. You never, ever hear someone say, 'I got too much attention as a child, they cared too much about me, they lavished attention on me, they listened too much.' You can't give your kids too much love."

The same principles apply to parents. As a parent, you must provide discipline and structure to your teenager, but you should also be sensitive to his needs for patience, latitude, and acceptance.

SIGNALS FROM DOGS AND TEENAGERS

The lessons learned about dealing with teenagers do not all come from academic research or child psychology. There are many real-life practical encounters that apply as well.

For example, I returned home after a week-long business trip recently to an interesting and insightful episode with my family. After greeting my husband, my son, and our dog Fergie, I dived into the stack of tasks waiting for me: emergency grocery shopping (doesn't anyone else ever buy milk?), washing clothes, sifting through the pile of mail for important bills, and unpacking. In the midst of this activity, Fergie stole my shoe.

After chasing her around the room, I retrieved it and scolded her, although she did look sort of cute as she held the loafer gently in her mouth, impishly threatening to eat the tassel.

A few minutes later, Fergie appeared with my son Ted's T-shirt in tow. (It was on the floor.) She wanted to be chased again. As soon as she dropped the T-shirt, I saw her lunge for a plastic hanger in the bottom of the closet, bent on destruction of forbidden items. She needed attention, and was rebelling against the rules, risking almost certain punishment but apparently satisfied that even negative attention was better than none.

Teenagers express the same needs for attention, and sometimes use the same vehicle of misbehavior to command it. If parents don't respond, the teenagers of Generation Risk do something bigger to get attention, and they find a way to make parents respond.

Fergie doesn't communicate with our family using spoken words. This inability puts her in the same boat as many teenagers, who are reluctant to communicate with their families, but for different reasons. Teenagers may be inhibited about discussing sensitive issues with their parents.

The limitations on verbal communication with Fergie don't stop her from making her wishes known most of the time. As humans, the members of our family respond at different rates to her signals, but generally we understand when she wants to go out, when she is hungry, and when she needs attention. It's not really too hard to guess what she needs at a given time, because the range of choices is fairly limited, and she becomes increasingly demonstrative as her needs intensify, especially if she feels she is being ignored.

In a sense, these are the same basic needs that apply to teenagers. They want to go out, they are hungry, and they need attention. Even though they may not tell us what they need at a given moment in words, there are usually other signals we can detect if we are vigilant about watching for them. If not, the intensity of the signals is likely to increase.

Dogs can't hide their emotions. When we show them love, dogs respond openly. Teenagers are more circumspect, but their feelings are not so different. Use your dog as a reminder that your teenager is dependent on you not only for food, water, and shelter, but also for affection, attention, and approval. These are the best tools you have for bonding with your teenager.

COMMUNICATION, NOT CONFRONTATION

Most teenagers would rather be thrown into a pit of cobras than be forced to talk to their parents about their personal lives. Teenagers writhe at the prospect of parental interrogation sessions and complain that parents are judgmental, close-minded, and dictatorial.

Joe

Joe was out late last night at a party. He doesn't really feel like talking right now. In fact, he'd rather be back in bed. A short stubble is growing on Joe's chin and around the edges of his face. He is wearing knee-length shorts, a pale green sweatshirt, and tan deck shoes. Around his neck is a string of beads. Joe is twirling one of the beads with his fingers and looking down at his feet.

"Why is it difficult to talk to my parents? My parents and I, we communicate. I just don't have that much open communication with them. I never know what to expect when I ask permission to go out with my friends or something. My mom and dad are like werewolves; they have different phases. I can't even predict anymore. Maybe I'll ask to spend the night out with one of my friends, and they'll start in on why didn't I cut the grass yet or something totally unrelated. My parents have such judgmental views on all my friends. I try not to bring anybody over. My mom is like, 'Oh, wow! I don't think you should hang out with them. They're from, like, Berkeley or something. I bet they smoke pot and stuff.' I don't need that kind of confrontation."

Teenagers say they'd love to be able to talk openly with their parents, but they rarely do, because communicating with parents too often ends up feeling like a grilling.

Holly

Holly is fifteen. She lives with her parents and her younger brother in a suburban neighborhood near the high school. Her father sells insurance. Holly has blonde hair, a heart-shaped face, and deep blue eyes. She is popular with the boys at her school. Holly loves to talk on the phone, and she loves to shop.

"I'll ask, 'Can I stay out late?' Then I have to go through an interrogation. They'll say, 'Where are you going? Who are you going to be with? What're their phone numbers? We want their addresses, social security numbers.' I'd rather not even go out. They're gonna ask a million questions. They might ask, 'Why are you doing this?' I wanted to do it. They ask a whole lot of questions they don't really need to know."

The teenagers of Generation Risk don't want to be grounded, punished, or cut off from their friends, so the easiest recourse is to limit communication with parents. If every discussion with parents feels like a cross-examination, these teenagers are likely to require a subpoena to appear.

Drew

Drew has a part-time job as a checker at the Winn-Dixie store a few miles from his house. Drew is looking forward to his high school spring break when he and his friends are going to South Padre Island for a few days on their own. He is wearing a navy hooded sweatshirt, faded jeans that are frayed at the cuffs, and brown leather shoes with large rubber-cleated soles.

"I can tell my mom the things I do, and at the moment she'll tell me her opinion. Then a couple of days later, she'll use it against me. So I'd rather not tell her anything. I'd rather just keep it to myself. I can't talk to my dad about anything, period. He has no clue about what's going on in reality, and I can't reason with him. He asks me, 'Why don't you ever talk to me?' I'm like, 'Because I know what your answer is going to be.' What does he think?"

Even worse than failing to relate to teenagers, many parents steer conversations to unpleasant topics such as a teenager's failure to complete chores or schoolwork, lack of consideration for others, or other shortcomings. The teenagers of Generation Risk have more exciting and enjoyable things to do than listen to these criticisms.

Joe

Joe is leaning back in his chair now and stretching his legs. His fingers are interlocked behind his head, and his sweatshirt is riding up, revealing his stomach. Drew leans over and pokes Joe in the ribs, and they begin to scuffle. When they settle down again, Joe continues to talk about his father.

"Sometimes I try to talk about what I'm doing, like when I'm trying to complete a model. I say, 'Yeah, Dad, where do I put this carburetor in the car?' He'll talk about that and then he'll kind of drift off the subject, then on to my grades, and then on to my attitude, and then on to all my negatives. I think, 'Oh, great. Here we go again.' It's a nightmare."

HOW TO REACH GENERATION RISK

Parents are not alone in the quest to break through to teenagers. Advertisers who market to teenagers realize the huge financial potential of this emerging population segment and routinely conduct research to determine what sort of messages reach them most effectively. Coincidentally, this information could be instructive to parents. What advertisers have learned from teenagers themselves is that teens don't need extraordinary techniques or shock value to get them to pay attention. *They want simple, direct communication.* In a recent survey conducted by Teenage Research Unlimited, teenagers gave their advice about how they can be reached. These excerpts from the top ten "Most Important Rules to Follow When Advertising to Teens" are surprisingly moderate:

- Be original.
- Don't try too hard to be cool.
- Say something important.
- Don't talk down to me.
- Don't tell me what to do.
- Be funny—make me laugh.
- Be honest.
- Be clear, so I get the message.

Teenagers want their parents to show this same sort of interest. What disappoints teens is parents who don't really pay attention and can't relate to the realities of teenage life today. What drives them away is confrontation and lack of respect.

THERE'S LISTENING, AND THERE'S REALLY LISTENING

The ability to listen well is a difficult skill to acquire. Parents typically don't attribute good listening skills to children: "Roger, how many times have I told you not to slam the screen door?" Many of us are guilty in day-to-day interactions of just "waiting to talk" instead of really listening. Marriage counselors are inundated with complaints about spouses who "just don't listen." And there are entire business programs on the subject of "active listening" that teach the art of concentrating on what's being said instead of planning what to say next.

It should come as no surprise that one of the biggest complaints teenagers express about their parents is a lack of listening.

Kristin

Kristin's long brown hair is parted in the middle and hooked behind each ear, well clear of her mouth, which is busily packing away a snack of Reese's Peanut Butter Cups. She is taking very small but rapid bites, like a hungry chipmunk. Kristin lives with her mother and younger sister in a duplex just down the street from the convenience store where her mother works part-time. Kristin is fourteen and wants to be a veterinarian.

"The thing that irritates me is when my mom says, 'How was your day?' or something. She doesn't really want to hear about my day. She doesn't want to be there and listen to me. She must just think she's supposed to ask. Parents scream and yell and think that that's the end of it. They automatically assume that they have the upper hand and they are just, 'Boom, boom, boom. Conversation, conversation.' You can't even get a word in. When I tell my mom something, she wants to interrupt me. She makes me lose my train of thought and she criticizes what I say. I don't know. My mom freaks out over every little thing, so now I don't tell her anything. If you tell your parents something, they'll make a bigger deal out of it than what it really is. I don't feel comfortable talking to my mom because she's my mom, and I'm embarrassed. I can talk to my aunt instead. You know, my mom says, 'You can always talk to me.' But you feel embarrassed."

This problem is magnified by the apparent compulsion of parents to provide advice, criticize behavior, and pick the worst possible moments to have conversations with their teenagers.

Teenagers would really like to talk to their parents, and they would do it more often if they felt confident about the results. Many teenagers say that the time they spend talking to their parents is not really very personal, but they wish that it could be. Others who have achieved some degree of open communication seem to value and appreciate not so much the advice they receive, but the knowledge *that somebody is there to talk to.* The teenagers of Generation Risk yearn for connections with parents. When they have the opportunity to speak freely without fear of punishment, they will initiate discussions with parents. But these discussions have to be *when teenagers feel comfortable talking.*

Adam

Adam has large feet. His size twelve basketball shoes seem to fill the room all by themselves, especially since he is propping them up on the chair next to him as he leans back and clasps his hands behind his head. Adam is sixteen, and wants to buy himself a car. He works part-time at McDonald's and plays sports.

"It's always like, just when I'm ready to go out with my friends or some-thing. That's when they want to talk. Or when I'm really tired from school or basketball practice and I just want to chill and relax. It's gotta be right then. Yeah, it has to be when they want to talk. If I try to talk to my parents, and they're watching television or something, they're like, 'That's good.' I can tell that they're not really paying attention to me. It's in one ear and out the other."

If teenagers pick when to approach parents, the odds of open com-munication are higher.

Kenny

Kenny is about 5'8" and has medium-length dark brown hair combed back on the sides and on top. Kenny drives an old junker car that his friends call The Blue Bomber, but it's more rust-colored than blue. Anyway, he can always drive places when he and his buddies need to get somewhere like the mall or the drive-in. Kenny is sixteen. He is wearing a Budweiser baseball cap, a white T-shirt with the sleeves cut off at the shoulders, jeans, and black Reeboks.

"Well, sometimes I actually have successful conversations with my par-ents, but that's not too often. What happens when I do? Usually I start the conversations when I feel like it. They don't come up to me and say, 'Let's have a talk about sex.' Or maybe we're just doing something together, like going to a game, and a subject comes up and we just talk about it a little. I

mean, not for an hour. I don't like it when the whole point is this prearranged plan to have a 'meaningful conversation.' I'd rather, like, clean my room than have to sit through one of those."

If you want your teenager to feel comfortable communicating, it's important to be open and willing to concentrate on what he has to say. If you're watching television, turn it off; if you're just getting into bed, try to keep your eyes open for a few more minutes—this opportunity may not come again for a while. In the midst of the confusing and fast-paced world that surrounds them, the teenagers of Generation Risk need to be able to rely on having access to you and your counsel—when they want it. They need a chance to participate in two-way conversations. If you're available to them as often as you can be, that will be an incentive to them to make the effort.

The teenagers of Generation Risk are sometimes silenced by fear of embarrassment over bringing up sensitive subjects. Often it's the very subjects that are the most important and most threatening that are most avoided. The parents of Generation Risk have to find ways to open communications and build connections with these teenagers.

WHY DIDN'T YOU JUST ASK?

Often our attempts to have meaningful talks with our teenagers run aground in predictable ways. We shower them with unwanted advice that is just about as welcome as another gray sweater at Christmas. (I love to give my son gray sweaters. He looks really good in gray sweaters. They bring out the sparkle in his eyes. Never mind that he already has a drawer full of gray sweaters.) Many times we do not consider the other half of the partnership when we talk to our teens.

We should try asking their opinions about things a little more often. As parents, it's tough to gauge the right time to shift from being absolute caretakers and decision-makers regarding our kids to sharing some of the responsibilities (and privileges) with them. We don't ask infants what brand of baby formula they would like for dinner. We don't include toddlers in discussions about financial investments for their college educations. Later, when we are suddenly confronted with teenagers desperate for independence, freedom, and responsibility, we may be ill prepared to provide this type of latitude unless we have practiced and conditioned ourselves along the way.

One way to prepare for shared decision-making and then for delegation of responsibility is to discuss the subject with our kids, who have plenty of ideas to offer. By reaching agreement on the importance of granting freedom, parents and teenagers can form a bond of trust, and both parties win.

Many kids have already developed a strong sense of identity and self-image by the time they become teenagers. There are certain activities they enjoy, certain styles of dress they prefer, and particular values they share with their peer groups. These teenagers expect a certain level of freedom in their decision-making and want to be recognized for their ability to exercise good judgment.

Lilly

Lilly has pulled her wavy blonde hair back into a bun. She is wearing a black skirt and a red turtleneck sweater with open-toed platform shoes. Her nails are painted black. She has a small hoop earring just above her right eyebrow, and light eye makeup but no lipstick. Lilly is fifteen.

"Parents should give us some freedom. Either parents give us the freedom, or we're going to do things behind their backs. Don't try to put chains on us. Don't try to give us every single rule in the book, just to make sure we never do anything. Because eventually, we're going to be out on our own. The more your parents don't let you do, the more you're going to want to rebel. So the more freedom that they give you, the more you'll be like, 'Well, my parents are pretty cool.' When other kids are saying, 'God I hate my parents . . . they don't let me do anything,' you can say, 'Well, my parents let me do a lot and they trust me.'"

SO WHAT WOULD YOU SUGGEST?

A good way to learn how to reach teenagers is to ask for their suggestions. Teenagers often come up with good ideas. This phenomenon is surprising to many parents who continue to see their teenagers as children rather than recognize them as emerging adults. Teens have some advice for parents that involves openness, sensitivity, and the ability to listen. As part of a recent focus group research study, teenagers were asked how parents should communicate with them to be effective. The teenagers responded with a range of creative suggestions.

These things work:

• Sort of ask you.
• Be more calm about it.
• The best approach would be telling you matter-of-factly about the consequences, then you decide for yourself.
• Make jokes about it. Make us comfortable.
• Tell you with love.
• Praise you for you the good things you do.

These things don't work:

• Ordering you.
• Being really strict.
• Arguing, because it makes you feel upset.
• Getting mad.
• Not understanding after you tell them what they asked about.
• Punching, grabbing.
• No discussion, just punishment.
• Thinking your child has to be perfect.

The teenagers of Generation Risk are treated with respect by marketers who want their business. They are sought after by moviemakers, magazine publishers, advertisers, retailers, and designers. Their voices are heard on the Internet, in music, and on MTV. They want this same sort of recognition from parents. The teens of Generation Risk want their parents to acknowledge their evolving maturity, and not just to give negative commands.

IMPROVING THE PARENT-TEEN EXCHANGE

Assuming you have your teen's attention—perhaps you're in the car and the radio is actually off—how do you break through the communication "black out" to get a conversation going? Sometimes prying responses out of teenagers can be torturous. When kids are making the difficult transition to adulthood, they are likely to want to avoid revealing much about their feelings or their behavior to their parents. One-syllable responses to questions about the school day, for example, are typical. They are usually followed by attempts to escape.

Here is an example of one of those conversations I recently attempted with my teenage son, Ted.

> "How was your day, Ted?"
> "Fine."
> "Did you have your Spanish test today?"
> "Yes."
> "Do you think it went well?"
> [long silence]
> "Ted, do you feel like talking about your Spanish test?"
> "Um, do you think it would be okay if I went over to see Travis for a while before dinner?"

Because I have been formally trained on the topic of interviewing, I recognize some flaws in my technique: I opened with a "closed" question, one that could be answered "yes" or "no" or "fine." It's much better to ask a job applicant, for instance, an "open" question that requires some discussion, such as "Why are you interested in accounting?" Then the applicant typically responds with a sentence or two, revealing some values, beliefs, or character traits, and providing an opportunity for follow-up questions. "I've always been fascinated by accounting theory because of the orderliness it provides. I thrive on precision."

Despite our efforts at improving conversations, however, teenagers have a talent for closing even the most open of questions. If I were to ask Ted, "What are the most important qualities you look for in another person?" he would probably respond, "I dunno."

The problem is that teenagers don't want to be interviewed. They are not applying for jobs. They're just trying to get through what they consider to be an interrogation when parents try to display an interest in their lives and ask questions.

One technique that works better is to focus on neutral subjects such as sports, not personal subjects such as teenagers themselves, their behavior, their values, their decisions, their haircuts, or their choice of friends. It's much easier to work around to these topics if you start somewhere else, generally as far away as possible.

A good opening might be, "So what are the chances of the team winning divisionals?" This question can be adapted to any sporting event at any time, and almost always evokes a multiword response. Not only that, starting the sentence with the word "so" shows sensitivity to modern linguistic conventions versus a rigid adherence to proper grammar—a concession that can only work in your favor in communications with your teenager.

THE BEAR AND DUCKY BEE

There are other ways of encouraging positive communication with teenagers. Most of them are based on avoiding confrontation, but not ignoring issues. With younger children, many parents develop techniques for pointing out problems without always having to yell or scold.

About the time our daughter was a toddler, we happened upon a novel communication technique that could be called "stuffed animal transference."

When Natalie misbehaved, she used to punish her favorite stuffed animal: her Winnie-the-Pooh bear. She was continually admonishing him for her minor transgressions and warning him to "Be good!" Poor innocent Pooh received numerous undeserved scoldings and occasional spankings, most of them delivered by Natalie. Our daughter, in turn, was able to learn lessons while saving face.

As fledgling parents, my husband and I discovered that confrontations with Natalie were much less productive than confrontations with Pooh. When problems arose, it was easy to enlist Natalie's help in solving them if the blame could be shifted to the bear. Our little daughter joined enthusiastically in reprimands, warnings, boundary setting, and praising accomplishments attributed to her stuffed animal because her own ego was not in jeopardy.

Her self-esteem continued to develop as she internalized strong values and a sense of responsibility for her bear, herself, and later for her little brother. She emerged from adolescence with self-esteem firmly intact and a strong identity, in part because she helped establish the rules for herself.

Of course what works with one child will not necessarily work the same way with another. By the time our son Ted came along five years after Natalie, we thought we had refined the technique of disciplining stuffed animals. Ted's favorite was an adorable yellow duck named Ducky Bee.

This duck took on a whole new dimension of importance when little Ted reached the age of four. When faced with any sort of stressful situation, Ted began to speak "duck talk" and to communicate with the family through the personality of Ducky Bee. The duck received many admonishments from Ted and the rest of the family. In fact, Ducky Bee was dragged into so many confrontations nose-first that his beak had to be replaced by Mrs. Bezy, who cared for Ted and Ducky Bee on weekdays.

In retrospect, I think Ted benefited from the lack of head-on parental conflict just as Natalie had done so before him, even though he may have reacted differently.

"Good morning, Ted. Did you leave your toy truck on the stairs again?"

"I'm not Ted, I'm Ducky Bee. Quack. Quack. I won't leave my truck out anymore."

Ted internalized the lessons handed out to Ducky Bee by instinctively creating a pre-school version of role-playing. As a high-profile actor, Ducky Bee valiantly bore the weight of Ted's misbehavior on his fuzzy little head and shoulders. In turn, as a vulnerable little guy, Ted managed to absorb the content of warnings, corrections, instructions, scoldings and criticism without risking his own dignity and sense of self-worth.

This same concept applies to the teenagers of Generation Risk whose egos are on the line and who care so much about achieving independence and respect. It's vital that parents avoid the head-on confrontations and criticisms that make teenagers withdraw from communication altogether.

Many of my longer conversations with Ted, now that he is a teenager are centered around our dog Fergie, to whom Ted humorously attributes a range of misdeeds and character flaws: "Fergie's tired because she was out drinking beeeeeer with her friends last night." I interpret this sort of comment as an acknowledgment by Ted that he did not drink beer the night before with his friends. He is affirming his understanding that his father and I would disapprove of such behavior. So the comment is a joke, but maybe also an opportunity to actually enter into a conversation about whether some of his friends are drinking beer and how he's coping.

It's not easy to carry on serious conversations with teenagers. The deflection of attention to someone or something else can make it easier, because the consequences are less direct. Threatening to revoke Fergie's driver's license or ground her for a month if she is ever caught drinking underage is funny to us because she is a dog. It's a silly, symbolic ritual behavior, but it makes an important point. (This particular discussion becomes blurred when we factor in the difference in human years and "dog years" to try to determine Fergie's true eligibility.)

KEEPING THE CONVERSATION HIGHWAY OPEN

Getting involved with our teenagers is incredibly important. Staying involved is even more important. But to many parents, involvement is not easily accomplished with evasive, moody, defensive, vulnerable—in other words, "normal"—teenagers.

Many parents feel that conversations about important and sensitive subjects are uncomfortable for everybody involved, and so they minimize the time spent on these topics. Teenagers may not enjoy these discussions much, either, but conversations about sex, drugs, alcohol, smoking, suicide, and violence are important not only to have once, but also to reinforce and build upon later.

Michelle

Michelle's hair is beginning to turn frizzy from the humidity in the air. She hates that. She is gathering it into an elastic ponytail holder and putting it up off her neck.

"I think parents should sit down and have the marijuana talk and have the birds and the bees talk. But I don't think you should sit down in 2001 and say, 'Okay, we had that talk. Now that's over.' It's got to be, like, a daily thing. You have to talk to your kids about drugs and things. You show them, and you've got to give them examples. Don't sit down with them, bring it up, get it out of the way, and then never talk about it again. It needs to be in lots of conversations, and it has to be genuine, very genuine."

If you force your teenager to talk about serious issues when you feel like it but he or she doesn't, or assume absolute stances through "end of discussion" pronouncements, you risk blocking opportunities to communicate. It doesn't work to use your parental power without providing an opportunity for your teenager to understand your perspective—and without taking the trouble to understand his or hers.

The teenagers of Generation Risk appreciate sensitivity to their points of view and a willingness by parents to relax and to really listen. More time is needed to relate to each other than the average seven minutes a day mothers spend or five minutes a day fathers spend talking to their teenagers.

Kenny

Kenny's beeper is buzzing. He loves to feel that vibration in his hand as he checks the number on the display. Kenny is already feeling a slight adrenaline rush because soon he will have plans to do something instead of just sitting around.

"Kind of ease up. I mean, try and relate to your child. Interact with them, try and understand what they're going through. Just try to listen. Listen before you say anything. Try to understand. Don't just give your opinion. When my mom gets worked up, she doesn't want to listen to me. I'm like, 'Well, this is what I wanted to say,' and then my mom is like, 'No, we're done with this conversation. You know how I feel about it.' You're like, 'Well, you don't know how I feel about it.' I want a chance to say something, too."

The Importance of Staying Involved

Parents should not withdraw from teenagers just because communicating has become difficult. A number of researchers have put forward the thesis that an all-powerful teen culture has emerged as a societal subculture in constant conflict with adults. Parents who believe this notion are paralyzed in their relationships with their teenagers, feeling that their teenagers no longer want to spend time with them or listen to their ideas.

A healthy alternative to this interpretation of surging teenage independence and high-risk exploration is that teenagers are seeking a whole new range of ideas and experiences to bring back and enrich the family. To enable your teenager to grow in this way, you have to be open to allowing him some freedom and inviting him to share his experiences and emotions.

Because teenagers in the age of *Generation Risk* spend so much time away from their parents, you also need to be alert to danger signs and need to encourage your teenager to talk about issues and to seek parental counsel. There are many ways to give direction to teenagers without provoking them. My dad was an expert at giving advice and not making people feel obligated to accept it. That's the kind of advice teenagers really want from parents: take-it-or-leave-it advice, their choice, guidance but freedom.

The teenagers of Generation Risk really do want advice and guidance. The most poignant criticisms teenagers level at parents relate to lack of involvement. Teenagers who feel their parents are out of touch with them express a feeling of *underlying sadness and a wish for things to be different.*

Valerie

Valerie would like more than anything to be able to talk to her parents about her fear of being pregnant. She just doesn't know how.

"Our parents don't know anything that we go through every day. They think we just go to our classes. I can't really talk to either of my parents. With my dad, we've always been just like, 'Hi, person that lives in the house.' We don't even bother to talk at all. Sometimes you'll feel that your parents don't have enough time for you, and that's the saddest feeling."

This distance between teenagers and parents was described by one student in a Chicago suburb as the "hi-goodbye relationship," in which kids are left to cope with their difficult teenage years with little parental guidance. If all we do is provide food and shelter, we are treating our children more like tenants than family members. Researcher Patricia Hersch suggests this problem of superficial communication affects most teenagers in America, and that really *listening to teenagers* is key to solving the crisis of school violence.

Valerie

Valerie is looking away, and her eyes are filling with tears.

"When your parents don't respond to you and don't listen to you, you have to do something bigger to make them listen. Each time you do more."

A recent study among children in grades 3 through 12 and their parents, cited in Ellen Galinsky's book, *Ask the Children*, revealed an underlying conflict among this generation of teenagers struggling to be self-sufficient. Even though they want support from parents, explicitly asking for help "makes them feel little again." These kids want to be involved with their parents *and* to grow up.

Communicating with your teenager is absolutely vital. You cannot afford to have communications break down during these critical years. Your teenager is developing more sophisticated skills, and much of what you need to do in maintaining communication with him or her is exactly what you would do with an adult: express sincere interest, pay attention when he is talking, and respond without criticism. If something needs to be resolved, then negotiate in such a way that both of you come away with something you feel is important.

A key to communicating effectively with your teen is to let her signal "when." You can help create these opportunities by staying involved with your teen—going to his games, taking her to her music lessons, and thinking of special things you both like to do. If you prove to her that you are generally available when she needs you, then you'll find that the "when" comes more frequently, and you can sometimes steer the topic to something you feel needs to be said. You will also be building a foundation to help your teenager manage some of the frustrations she will inevitably face during the tumultuous years until adulthood.

7

AVOIDING THE NEED FOR RISKY BEHAVIOR: HELPING YOUR TEEN MANAGE STRESS AND ANGER

Kids pay full price to attend movies at age twelve. In most states, they can obtain a driver's license at age sixteen. They are allowed to serve in the military and to vote at age eighteen, but they aren't permitted to drink legally until age twenty-one. Most kids are handed the incredibly important responsibility of babysitting for neighbors or younger siblings by age twelve or earlier. Yet they may not rent a car from most companies until they are twenty-five. No wonder kids are confused when parents treat them as children in some ways, yet expect them to behave maturely in others.

"You think you're old enough to handle it. You're at that point where you're not a little kid, but you're not an adult," says Richard, a seventeen-year-old who wears a gold stud in his right nostril and a tattoo of a dragon on his left forearm. "If you're old enough to serve your country, how come you can't drink a few beers on the weekend? If you're old enough to work, you're making your own money, but you can't make your own choices on what you want to spend it on. It's frustrating."

The cloudiness around the rules doesn't end at home. Some school officials allow kids to smoke outside of the normal school day. At one local school in Louisville, for instance, smoking is allowed at school dances. How can adolescent smoking be a problem during school hours only? For teenagers eager to experience all the richness of life, it may seem that most age limits are meaningless barriers.

RISK BEHAVIOR AND STRESS

Teenagers are waiting to be old enough—for everything. Teenagers are waiting to be respected. Teenagers are angry about arbitrary rules that make them wait to participate in activities they want to experience. Parents have to be ready to address this frustration and to help ease the resulting anger.

Stress is part of everyday life, and it seems to increase with every generation. The electronic age has added a layer of frustration through the phenomenon of computerized voices and automatic answering machines. According to author Tom Heymann, Americans together average 101,369,863 hours per day waiting in line. For the teenagers of Generation Risk, there is an incongruous juxtaposition of waiting versus the high-speed immediacy of so much of their lives. Anthropologist David Murray explains that waiting is an insult, and that this insult leads to anger. Teenagers with fragile self-esteem are particularly susceptible to this brand of anger.

In her book, *The Culture of Adolescent Risk-Taking*, author Cynthia Lightfoot quotes teenagers who describe risk behavior as a way to relieve stress as well as rebel, test their freedom and limitations, and to show autonomy. Teenagers today need outlets for their frustrations, and one distressing alternative is violence.

VIOLENCE IS ALL AROUND

Our society is loaded with poor examples for teenagers to follow. In a recent national survey on teen violence three out of four teens said they believe that violent behavior is a learned behavior. In the same study,

386,000 teenagers reported carrying a gun for protection in the previous year. In a 1993 survey of high schools nationwide, nearly 12 percent of students reported carrying guns onto school grounds. In 1991, a U.S. Department of Justice survey reported 15 percent of students said gangs existed in their schools, and 16 percent said they had witnessed students threatening or attacking teachers. An average of sixty-five people die, and over 6,000 people are physically injured as a result of interpersonal violence in the United States each day.

Psychologist Albert Bandura's "Social Learning Theory" suggests that humans are not innately aggressive, but that they model observed behavior. This theory supports the assertion that media violence influences violent behavior. A 1990 report by the National Coalition on Television Violence cited that nine of twelve research studies on the impact of violent video games reported harmful effects on children. According to the FBI's Uniform Crime Reports and Census Bureau data, the rate of arrests for violent crimes among fourteen to seventeen year-olds increased over 46 percent from 1989 to 1994.

One theory that attempts to explain the popularity of hip-hop music proposes that this rebellious medium resonates with the natural emotions of teenagers who feel powerless in an adult world. The anger and outrage in hip-hop lyrics are interpreted as responses to feelings of adolescent anxiety, oppressions, and mistreatment. This evidence of growing anger and violence among teenagers cries out for parental intervention. Many of the teenagers of Generation Risk are angry. They are taking risks to relieve stress, and they are expressing their frustration in destructive ways. As a parent, it's time to pay attention to your teenager to defuse this ticking time bomb.

MANAGING ANGER AND STRESS

The most successful school-based programs to reduce violence and drug and tobacco use teach "social resistance skills." These programs provide junior high school and middle school students with the skills needed to resist peer pressure while maintaining friendships, and they appeal to the teenage desire to fit in with the group by pointing out that most kids are *not* using drugs or smoking. These programs are even more effective when combined with broader social skills training, including decision-making skills, goal setting, communication skills, assertiveness skills, general social skills, and *stress management.*

The American Psychological Association offers tips on managing anger that range from relaxation techniques to problem diffusion. For example, timing is considered an important element in handling anger. An option for handling anger is to postpone dealing with conflict until the heat of the moment passes. Another suggestion is avoidance, which means not exposing yourself to situations that you know will anger you. You might want to steer clear of your teenager's room if messiness irritates you. In the same way, you can help your teenager avoid areas of stress and conflict.

Controlling anger is another important skill. Instead of raging indiscriminately, parents need to demonstrate self-restraint in the face of anger. Handling anger appropriately gives teenagers a positive model to follow and avoids a number of family risk factors such as destruction of family bonds, unfair punishment, and antisocial behavior.

At other times, it's important to let feelings of anger out. For kids to learn how to express anger appropriately, parents need to act as models and establish norms of social behavior. You have to express your own anger in proportion to the problem. You have to be consistent. You have to be sure to keep your anger focused on the problem and never threaten family bonds even when you are furious. You have to understand that your teenager will be angry at times and will need to express that anger.

As an example, my son Ted was scheduled to spend a week in New Orleans visiting his older sister. Being a teenager, he put off packing until the last minute (the morning of the trip) and displayed what I would consider typical signs of anger when things did not go smoothly. I was out for an early morning run, leaving the packing to Ted and dealing with my own needs for stress relief.

When I arrived home, Ted was raging around the house in a fit of pique. He had left his backpack in his friend's van and could not find a suitable carry-on bag to stuff his clothes into for the week. Travis and his family (and Ted's backpack) were already en route to Florida in their van, and the zipper on Ted's old backup Nike bag was broken. He was enraged and frustrated, slamming doors and shouting at the dog.

When I gently inquired about what might be the problem, Ted

explained, adding with a note of desperation, "Dad's down at the coffee shop, you're out running, and I have to get to the airport. You guys never tell me when you're coming home, but I always have to tell you when I'm coming home!"

I volunteered to help find a substitute suitcase. "Suitcase?" Ted echoed in horror. "I need a backpack, not a suitcase!" So I volunteered to swing by Target on the way to the airport and pick up a new backpack, since the old one was falling apart anyway. This suggestion was actually a solution. Ted wasn't missing anything inside the backpack. A new backpack would be fine. The store was open; we had time to go there, and there was no reason for him to continue stomping around the house being angry. Oddly, though, that wasn't the end of it. Ted continued to frown, sulk, and grouse for at least another five minutes (which seemed longer). Then things were fine.

What struck me as interesting—and the point to this story—is that sometimes we need time to work through our anger, even when the rational causes for the anger are gone. Ted was still mad, even though the solution to the problem had been identified. He needed time to work through his feelings in order to regain his emotional equilibrium.

I have experienced this sort of frustration, too. I remember a particular example when I was upset with my daughter Natalie about something. I yelled about it, and she apologized. Then I yelled some more. She raised her voice in return with a tone of pure indignation and protested, "I said I was sorry." We were fighting at that point not about the original problem at all, but about the fact that I was not ready to let go of my anger. I had to yell some more, just to get it out of my system.

CONTROL YOUR OWN STRESS

To avoid increasing their frustration even more, we have to be sure not to take our stress and anger out on our kids. In a new study about parents, kids, and stress, author Ellen Galinsky reveals some important insights about the effects of parental stress. Kids were asked, "If you were granted one wish to change the way that your mother's/father's work affects your life, what would that wish be?" Most parents assumed their kids would wish for more time together. But only 10 percent of the kids wanted more time with their mothers, and only about 15 percent wanted more time with their fathers. In contrast, 34 percent said what they wanted most was for parents to be less stressed, or less tired, because of their work.

The stress parents feel at work clearly affects parenting behavior. Keeping these feelings separate is an essential step in treating teenagers fairly.

Change is stress, and individual stress translates to family stress. Teenagers are undergoing physical and emotional change almost daily. They are being thrust into new environments, surrounded by temptations, and disenfranchised from their value systems from the past. Just as adults become absorbed in new job assignments or personal crises and transfer their stress to others, teenagers are subjected to equally valid and demanding pressures, especially in the age of Generation Risk.

USE YOUR DOG AS AN EMOTIONAL BAROMETER

Parents sometimes need to find unconventional ways to detect and manage family stress. If you pay attention, you can use your family pet as an emotional barometer. Being a true dog lover, I will use the example of dogs, but the same thinking might apply equally to other types of pets. (If you have a preference for cats, even though I could never understand you, I still respect your right to choose, and I hope you can apply some of this dog logic to your own situation.)

Think about how your dog responds when you've had a particularly rough day. If you are grouchy and irritable, your dog will probably sense your mood and steer clear until you send a welcoming or at least a neutral signal. Dogs don't usually try to cuddle up to us if we are slamming doors, kicking chairs, and bashing countertops. (Cats may be even more evasive.)

My dog can become almost invisible on these days, slinking from the edge of one room to another just out of range, head ducked. But as soon as I show the slightest sign of balance (eye contact is one giveaway), she practically bounds over to me, wiggles excitedly at her good fortune at being forgiven (for whatever), and nuzzles and licks away whatever shred of anger remains.

One thing is really clear to me when I don't interact well with my dog: *it's not the dog's fault.* Now, this clarity does not exist in most relationships.

If you and your spouse snap at each other after a long day, how do you know whose fault it is? How do you pick the right moment to resolve the conflict? Or if you find yourself in conflict with your teenager, how do you know whether you might have provoked the argument? With a dog, it's simple. It's never the dog who picks a fight, and the dog is always ready to make up.

So a good test of your own equanimity is to interact with your dog, just to determine whether you yourself at that moment happen to be spoiling for a fight. If you can't get along with your dog, do something to work the tension out of your system. Wrestle with the dog. Play tug-of-war with a dish towel or a toy. Go out for a run together. Work it out. Then interact with your teenager, without bringing conflict to the relationship.

My interaction with my dog is a metaphor for life. She provides an example of how others respond to shortness and irritation versus a kinder tone of voice and a more gentle demeanor. She instinctively knows that her categorical, unconditional love can break through any temporary barrier between us.

It's the same with parents and teenagers. Unconditional love doesn't mean we can't get angry, that we can't make rules and set boundaries. It means that after the smoke clears, whatever the subject of a conflict, what remains is a rock-solid bond of caring and affection.

RULES OF ENGAGEMENT

Besides being careful not to let the stress in our lives spill over into our relationships with our teenagers, we also have to be fair and to abide by certain rules to control anger when we deal with our kids.

Lincoln

Lincoln is really irritated. He ordered three CDs over the Internet, and only one of them was delivered correctly. One was the wrong title, and the other was a two-disk set with one of the disks missing. Lincoln is sitting at the table with his arms folded across his chest, scowling at the rest of the group. He is wearing athletic pants and a Life is Full of Choices T-shirt with different brands of beer printed across the front. Lincoln is seventeen.

"Parents hold grudges. There was one time that I came home at midnight. They never let that go, and that was like when I was eleven. They're always, 'Do you remember the time you came home at midnight? I was so worried. How do I know that you won't do it again? How do I know you won't get into more trouble this time?' My dad, he'll be mad for a month, and if it comes up again, he'll get mad again. It's ridiculous, because my parents still bring things up from seventh grade, and now I'm a junior. 'Well, you know, you did this.' Okay—four years ago. You know, that's what really makes me upset is when they bring up that stuff."

There are certain rules that should be followed when we fight with each other, especially within families. (Spouses should think about these things, too.) These rules focus our anger on specific actions and situations and not on each other, and they help us recover without permanent damage to our relationships. Teenagers are especially frustrated and angry when they feel that they are being treated *unfairly*.

Rule #1: Leave archaeology to the scientists.

It's pretty easy to dig up the bones of old arguments over and over again, but all we accomplish when we do so is to open old wounds. For example, if your teenager once lied to you about where he was going, you should resolve that problem and then bury it. It won't help to bring it up again next time you doubt his story. If you do, then he may think that he can never recover from having lied in the past, and he may be discouraged from even trying. If a given problem is serious enough to deal with, then it should stand on its own and be handled on its own. Once problems are resolved, they should be filed away.

Rule #2: Get angry at the behavior, not at the person.

When we attack a person's character, we risk saying things we don't really mean. Cutting remarks are not easily forgotten. If you call your teenager "stupid," she may think you don't respect her intelligence or her judgment. If you say instead that she made a "stupid decision," you can still achieve the same amount of emotional release for yourself, but her ego will not be battered in the process.

Rule #3: Allow enough time for the steam to condense.

If we are boiling hot when we are angry, then we should remember that steam can burn. We have to give each other enough time to cool down even after problems are resolved. Often it helps to delay discussing a problem until the worst of your anger has blown over and you have a chance to talk things through calmly.

Rule #4: Keep a mirror handy.

It's pretty easy to see the mistakes that other people are making. If one of your family members is violating Rules #1, #2, or #3, it will probably be very visible to you. But if you are the one who isn't fighting fairly, it may be harder to see. The angrier you feel, the more blurred your vision may be. So it's helpful to try to step outside yourself and take as objective a look as possible at how you are behaving. If you look like an infuriated lunatic, then you are probably not handling the situation in the best way.

Learning to Chill Out

There's an old adage from a Dale Carnegie speaking course my dad once attended that applies here. When he was a young man, my dad needed to develop more self-confidence. He was approaching his work with good natural instincts but without formal training in public speaking, and he didn't think he was coming across with enough enthusiasm to his customers.

The course instructor said, "*Act enthusiastic, and you'll be enthusiastic.*" Sure enough, when my dad tried his next speech (about which he was feeling a lot more nervous than enthusiastic), he interjected more emotion and visible signs of zeal, and the result was terrific. He was not only more convincing to his audience, but he also felt better about himself. He couldn't help truly feeling enthusiastic about his subject because he was transmitting the vocal inflections, facial expressions, and body language that an enthusiastic person would exhibit, and they affected him as well as his audience.

In managing our anger, we can apply the rule, *Act calm, and you'll feel calm.* If you think about how you look to your teenager, there's a better chance you'll control not only your outward appearance but also your inner emotions.

Teenagers want to be treated with respect and much prefer to deal with parents who are not yelling and screaming.

Monica

Monica plays the piano. She loves classical music, especially Beethoven, and wants to be a concert pianist. Monica thinks about music when she wants to relax, because it puts her in complete control of her emotions. She is becoming irritated with the rest of the group because they are wasting time. There has been too much horsing around and there have been too many dumb comments to please her. Monica is sixteen, but feels older. She thinks that most of the other kids in the room are acting like babies.

"The best way to give us direction actually is to tell us calmly, 'If you do that, you'll suffer my wrath.' Arguing won't help. Arguing doesn't do anything but make you mad. If you just talk the situation out without arguing, it helps a whole lot. Basically, if you're just yelling, you're saying things because you're mad. You don't even know what you're saying. When you're talking, you're calm and you're just talking. Don't interrupt and raise your voice really loud because if you start yelling, the kids ignore you from there on. They'll tune you out. They won't listen to what you have to say."

The pent-up frustration inside these kids can bubble over at the slightest provocation. Teenagers today are used to having free access to all varieties of activities and material goods, from drugs to cigarettes to alcohol. When they are denied something—anything—they can erupt. The violence that surrounds them sets a standard of outrageous behavior and unchecked emotions that they perceive as normal. It's up to you as a parent to establish a positive frame of reference to manage the anger of Generation Risk. In addition to managing household stress in the best manner possible, it's a good idea to give your teen a little more control where you can.

Our society has judged that teenagers are not ready to make certain decisions on their own, that they should still rely on the judgment of adults to help them settle on reasonable and appropriate courses of action. But for teens themselves, the sheer frustration of being refused permission can overwhelm their appreciation of a responsible adult's cautious advice.

If you want your advice to be heeded, you have to establish a base of credibility with your teenager. You have to build trust and mutual understanding. You have to provide reasons why you are suggesting or requiring certain behaviors. You shouldn't expect yourself to be an expert at this kind of work, so you should be open to some suggestions, even (or especially) from your teenager.

Julie

Julie is eating M&Ms from the candy bowl in the middle of the table. She began with a small taste, then she scooped out a handful and arranged them by color in rows on the table in front of her. She is eating one row at a time. She is working on the blues. Julie is fourteen, and feels restricted by her parents. She doesn't understand why they make up so many rules to limit her fun.

"When they're just like, 'Don't,' and you have no idea why, that makes you mad and makes you want to do it because you just don't understand what they're talking about. How come? It's like, if they told you, then it wouldn't be a big deal, but the fact that they're just commanding makes you want to. You need to understand things sometimes. When you're five and your parents tell you not to do things, you rely on them, so pretty much everything they say goes, and you have no choice. But the older you get, the more freedom you have, and the more questions you have, so the more you need reasons just to understand why they're telling you not to do something."

STAY INVOLVED

It's easy for busy parents to fall out of touch with teenagers. It's tempting to let the pressures of modern society block opportunities for interaction. But trends in violence and risk prove that it's more important than ever to stay involved with our teenagers so that we are there to recognize and manage the stress and anger they feel.

A Temple University study of 20,000 high school students found a significant lack of involvement in their teenagers' lives among nearly 30 percent of the parents interviewed. These parents were unable to explain how their teenagers spent their time or to name their teenagers' friends. Without involvement, parents have little chance of spotting warning signs of problems.

Research shows that teenagers who are alienated from parents are more susceptible to academic problems, mental health problems, and behavioral problems. Staying connected to parents during the teenage years is the best protection social scientists have ever been able to find for kids. Just as one example taken from Harvard Medical School psychologist William Pollack's work, "a positive dinner with your teenager three times a week brings the chances of suicide, depressions and aggressive behavior down dramatically." That's not much to ask from a parent.

You can find ways to get involved and stay involved with your teenager. The more p*ositive* time you spend together, the better. If you have limited time to be with your teenager, be sure to take advantage of opportunities for positive interaction.

Sit down together for dinner with your teenager at least three times a week, or go out together for a few meals.

There's something innately relaxing about the process of eating a seated meal. Instead of rushing off in different directions, interact over dinner and institutionalize the process of sharing your feelings or describing encounters. Chew slowly, listen to your teenager, and savor your time together. Remember what you talked about during the last meal, and continue your discussions. Show an interest in what your teenager is doing and feeling.

Tell your teenager about your day.

Being involved with your teenager doesn't have to mean asking probing questions. Act as a role model by revealing events in your own day that were interesting, frustrating, enlightening, pleasing, or otherwise significant. Describe the personalities of people you see regularly, and encourage your teenager to share in the same way about friends and teachers.

Ask for her advice about something in your life.

Let your teenager know you value her opinion by describing a problem and saying, "*What do you think I should do?*" Follow your teenager's advice whenever you can, and report back on the results.

Attend his sports practice, game, recital, or play.

Show that you are interested in your teenager's extracurricular activities. If you *aren't* interested in the activities, attend occasionally anyway to show that you are interested in your *teenager*. Demonstrate that you are willing to endure some inconvenience in your life to show support.

Go somewhere together in your car.

Take advantage of the fact that you are together in your vehicle with your teenager, at least for a short period of time. Resist the temptation to lecture, harangue, or quiz your "captive audience." Introduce positive topics. Give your teenager a chance to talk about his feelings and his friends.

Rent a movie together. Then talk about it.

Reflect on the values expressed in a movie as well as the plot, performances, and special effects. Let your teenager describe his reactions. Notice which characters he seems to admire and which ones he criticizes. Such characteristics and behaviors may give you some insight into your teenager's values or the pressures he faces.

Find something to laugh about together.

Do your best to make your teenager's time with you enjoyable. Find topics to discuss that are amusing. Remember things you've done together that were fun or funny. Rekindle positive associations you have shared. Allow yourself to have a good time.

A large proportion of the influences on children in their early years comes from parents and other adults. As teenagers, however, their peer groups will exert increasing influence. If we recognize that our opinions do not carry the same weight with our teenagers as they used to, because we are competing with peer groups, popular culture, the natural needs of teenagers to rebel, and teenage stress and anger, we may be able to avoid the conflict that often develops between parents and teens. Instead of driving a verbal wedge between us by behaving as authoritarian parents and adding to our teenager's stress and frustration, we can find alternative ways of communicating the rules and resolving issues.

ENEMIES OF RISK: DISCIPLINE, RESPONSIBILITY, AND MUTUAL TRUST

If I'm more of an influence to your son as a rapper than you are as a father . . . you got to look at yourself as a parent.
—Ice Cube

No matter how strong the influence of popular culture, parents are still central figures in the lives of their teenagers. Parents play the key role in engendering values, establishing boundaries, and building stability. One of the first and most enduring responsibilities of a parent is to provide discipline. For the teenagers of *Generation Risk*, this basic building block in the parent-child relationship is crucial because discipline provides a model for self-discipline.

SPARE THE ROD AND SPOIL THE CHILD

When parents discipline children, boundaries are defined. Even though children might not like it while it's being applied, they can understand why disciplinary action is needed. Later, they will appreciate this essential contribution to their character development. Teenagers often relate stories of "getting caught" or "getting busted" by parents and benefiting from the experience.

Carson

Carson is fourteen and is thinking about getting a dirt bike. His friend Kevin has a dirt bike and always gets to ride it on weekends at his uncle's farm. Carson is wearing a gray T-shirt, a pair of swimming trunks, and sandals. His light brown hair is parted in the middle and cut short. His face and arms are tanned, and his eyebrows are bleached blond from the sun. He has spent most of the summer at the neighborhood pool.

"Once me and a bunch of my friends were sitting there smoking cigarettes. My mom came in and said, 'Is that cigarette smoke?' Me and Mom had a fight about that after my friends left. It was a bad situation in a way and a good situation in a way. My mom gets on my nerves telling me, 'You have to do this and that,' but it's good that she does. I'm glad that she does, even though I argue with her sometimes and tell her to leave me alone."

It is not unusual for teenagers to appreciate the efforts of parents to establish and maintain discipline. In the age of Generation Risk, surrounded by opportunities to be reckless and prodded by the expectations of their peer groups, many teenagers long for parental intervention. These emotionally overloaded teenagers may engage in certain dangerous activities just to test whether parents are paying attention.

Bailey

Bailey is sitting at the table, folding and unfolding a piece of paper. His cell phone is hooked to his belt with a small swivel clip. Bailey is wearing an oversized white T-shirt, khaki shorts, hiking boots, and a white wristband on his right arm. On his left wrist is a bracelet made of pea-sized green and orange marbled beads, and next to it is a large silver-colored diver's watch, waterproof to 650 feet. Bailey is fifteen. He has never been diving.

"When you take a risk, it's good to get caught by your parents. I was drinking in my house, and my dad walked in. He came home early or something. I've never done it since. I think, if you have at least one strong parental figure in your life, you'll turn out fine. Some kids don't have enough discipline. Their parents don't teach them good morals. I've seen parents just try to be their kids' best friends and let them do whatever they want, and it screwed up their lives because they've had no guidance and no path to follow. If you let your kids do whatever they want because you want them to like you, what makes you think they're going to listen to you when they're older?"

Teenagers understand the role of discipline and expect it from responsible parents. They attribute the wild behavior of some of their peers to a lack of structure and needed control by parents. In many cases exercising parental discipline creates positive feelings among teenagers, because they recognize that discipline stems from caring. Parents may think they are doing kids a favor to give them free rein, but the teenagers of *Generation Risk* need to know their parents are concerned about where they are and what they're doing.

One well-researched disciplinary model distinguishes parents as authoritative, authoritarian, or permissive, and has measured the impact of these styles on teenage behavior. Authoritative parents provide a structured environment with well-defined and clearly communicated limits. They hold their children responsible but give some leeway to experiment and make mistakes. Children of authoritative parents are the most likely to be successful in almost all aspects of their lives. In contrast, authoritarian parents are rigid in their expectations, and permissive parents back away from discipline and structure. Neither of these approaches is as effective as the first.

Start Early

It's never too early to start instilling discipline in children. You owe it to yourself, to your children, and to the people around you.

My friend Joan told me about an airplane trip that pushed her to the brink recently. She sat in front of a young child who repeatedly banged the back of her seat with his GI Joe toy. Neck-craning, glaring, and throat-clearing hints were apparently too subtle for either the child or his mother, so finally Joan asked the parent to please control her unruly child. "*I will not*," said the mother. "*You have to understand that he's only five years old.*"

Joan had a different point of view. Fortunately the parent was smart enough to change seats with her son before an open fight broke out. But apparently this parent did not acknowledge the need to conform to the societal norms of airplane travel.

Flying normally heightens our sensitivity to those around us. Because everybody is trapped in a confined space, some fearing disaster, others simply irritated about inevitable delays and inconveniences, people owe it to each other to behave in a slightly different manner as airplane passengers than on solid ground.

Teaching kids to adapt to the rules of airplane etiquette really means explaining that there are different, more intense expectations in this new environment. In order to be successful, you can't start instilling discipline in your child just as the flight begins. You have to build upon a base of understanding that's been established over time. So when Mommy says to play quietly, the child has to understand that there is an expectation that he will in fact play quietly, and that there will be consequences to be faced if not.

In the same way, you can't just begin as the parent of a teenager to establish rules. You have to work your way through the transitional adolescent years by building upon trust established over time. As a teenager, and particularly as a member of Generation Risk, your child will be faced with a whole new environment, not unlike hurtling through the air at hundreds of miles per hour. You have a chance to build some basic flying skills before the plane takes off. Start by instilling discipline.

TAKE RESPONSIBILITY

At a certain point, parents must let teenagers make their own decisions. One technique for preparing for this day is to gradually give them certain responsibilities and let them slowly construct the elements of strong character and good citizenship. For example, kids can participate in setting boundaries for their own behavior, such as reasonable curfews. They can help decide what their roles should be in handling the family chores. They can control a certain amount of money designated for their own entertainment, and they can learn to manage a budget by counterbalancing quality versus quantity in their choice of clothes.

On the other hand, there are certain jobs that a responsible parent must retain. Parents still need to monitor teenagers to ensure their well being, to exert some measure of control, and to impose some level of discipline, so these kids know the rules are important. But judging when to allow freedom and when to exert disciplinary control can be a difficult task.

Years ago, when our son Ted was about five years old, he was feeling angry and destructive one afternoon. He had taken the broom handle and bashed it repeatedly against the screened-in sections of the back porch, creating huge gouges in the screens, yelling and stamping his feet all the while. The tantrum subsided when Dad came storming onto the back porch in response to all the racket. Ted had no option but to admit that he was the source of the property damage.

Ted was quaking. He had been caught red-handed and knew that he was in big trouble. He expected to be punished. For some reason, possibly because Ted looked so worried, my husband decided to let our son determine his own punishment. I can still remember the look on Ted's face as he stood there, silently considering all the known possibilities. Finally a tiny sound emerged from the wretched being in front of us. Ted suggested with utter seriousness, and without understanding the slightest thing about what he was saying, "*Grounded?*"

At age five, our son had nothing to be grounded from. He had no social life, no privileges, and no phone calls to disallow. Although he didn't intend it to be so, it was the perfect punishment, because he lost nothing. We ended up forgiving Ted with a stern warning, and we learned that some responsibilities are better left to parents.

ALL THE ANSWERS

I learned some important lessons from parenting our daughter as well. When Natalie was two years old, I used to drive her to her Mini-School day care center every morning, and we would talk about important topics such as animal sounds.

"What does a duck say?" I would ask.

"Quack, quack," she would answer.

"Yes, Natalie. That's wonderful." I would continue, "What does a cow say?"

"*Mooooo*," she would respond.

Sometimes she would ask the questions. "What does a turkey say, Mommy?"

"Gobble, gobble, Sweetheart."

We progressed pretty smoothly through ducks, pigs, donkeys, and frogs. This game was fun for both of us, and educational for my little daughter. Then one day she stumped me with, "Mommy, what does a turtle say?"

I was silenced. I simply didn't know the answer to this basic question from a two-year-old child. I still don't know what a turtle says.

This experience was good preparation for me for Natalie's upcoming teenage years. I realized there would be literally thousands of questions to come for which I had no answers.

As the parent of a teenager, you can't expect to have answers for many of the questions your child will face. When you were a teenager, you may never have experienced the kinds of pressures that bombard today's teenagers of Generation Risk to use drugs, smoke cigarettes, engage in sex, drink alcohol, or join gangs.

Most wisdom in life comes from personal experience, or something close. We have lived it, read it, heard it, felt it, learned it, seen it, or otherwise experienced whatever is at issue. That experience gives us a basis of authority from which to speak in guiding our children.

But when your kids are faced with challenges that are out of your comfort zone, when you can neither tell stories about what you did right in this situation or what you did wrong, how can you help them? What if you don't have any wisdom to impart?

The answer is that you still have to take responsibility for helping. Whether you have all the answers or not, you must act on your best judgment to set appropriate limits for your teenagers just at the time when they are most wanting freedom instead.

Mattie Mack: Kentucky Farmer

A brief visit to Brandenburg, Kentucky, just off the Ohio River near the Indiana border can help explain how responsibility and discipline work together. Picture this scene:

You've just worked your way through the five mongrel dogs that greeted you as you drove up to the Mack farm. The horses in the field to your left are looking at your car curiously, probably hoping you've brought apples as Mattie always does. You can hear Mattie Mack coming toward the door as you stand out in the Kentucky sunshine at the edge of her front porch swing.

"I'm comin', I'm comin' right now. You just come on inside and let's talk now."

Mattie Mack is a farmer, an outspoken advocate on the subject of personal responsibility, and a mother through and through. Her face beams with good humor when she talks about her farm, her dogs, and her horses. But her real pride is in her children.

She is wearing a brightly flowered blouse and a checkered skirt that billows around her ample body. She moves with determination and authority, establishing within minutes that she is the pillar of her family and a dominant force in her universe, an African-American matriarch who has overcome challenges most of us would shudder to face.

Her smooth face settles into a picture of intensity when she expounds on her views of what's missing in the interaction between parents and children today. She believes in establishing rules and maintaining discipline, and her booming voice and riveting eyes convince you that she means business. Her kids all knew it, too, and now her grandchildren are learning to live by her abiding values.

Mattie raised four children and thirty-eight foster children, and she has some things to say about discipline and responsibility. She prides herself on years of dealing with children as a strong family figure. She taught them responsibility by expecting them to be reliable and to use good judgment. If they lived up to their commitments, they were rewarded with more freedoms. If they didn't, they lost ground—and quickly. Mattie believed in spelling out expectations and giving kids specific chores to do around the house. "You tell those kids just what you expect from them. You give them jobs to do and make sure they do them real well, and see that they study their lessons."

Mattie put rules on paper to make them clear and visible. She took her kids to the county jailhouse to show them the consequences of breaking the law, and she let them see and smell and feel the coldness of a prisoner's cell. She made sure that the law, meaning a clear framework of expectations and consequences, was ingrained in her kids day and night. "Yes, that's right, my children worked by the law; they ate the law; they slept on the law; and they wore the law," she explains, "They knew what was right, and they were expected to follow those rules."

Mattie's children and foster children knew what was expected of them. She never ducked responsibility as a parent. She had a clear view of who was accountable for providing guidance for her kids, from the moment they came into her home. "It's not the government's role. It's the parents' role. The preacher can't do it all; the Sisters in the church can't do it all. It's going to have to be the parents to bring these kids along and to teach them right from wrong. It's the parents."

Mattie Mack's philosophy was to start early and communicate often with her children. She took every opportunity to explain and emphasize, to clarify and embed values. She began from the first day with each child. "You have to start with a child very small to instill in them what's right and wrong. And you have to start when you bring those little fellows home."

Mattie showed she could also profoundly influence foster children, many of whom came to her as teenagers. She believes adamantly in the importance of sitting down and talking with your children, regardless of when you begin. "It's never too late. Never too late.", she says, "Just keep on telling them and make them know in their hearts that 'this is the right thing to do.' You won't be sorry."

SCHOOLS CAN HELP

Many parents feel overwhelmed by the pressures of modern society and look to the educational system to help their children develop values and skills. Broadly speaking, our school systems are not equipped to fulfill this role as they struggle to meet the educational needs of students while maintaining discipline and suppressing violence.

Yet some educators and schools are developing novel methods to meet the challenges of Generation Risk. They recognize that this new generation of children is exposed to increasingly complex issues and that revolutionary methods are needed to enable these kids to cope. One such program is found in Kentucky—the Goshen Elementary School. The principal, Chris Lavisi, explains some of the concepts behind his approach to education, which is centered upon building a sense of community.

"Our focus is on character-education issues. Each month we take an idea and focus on it as a school: responsibility, teamwork, caring, confidence, motivation, effort, initiative. Every day the teachers reinforce those concepts, and that's part of a school-wide guidance program."

Principal Lavisi credits some of the ideas used in his school to Dorothy Rich's book, *MegaSkills*, published in 1992. The program at Goshen Elementary is constantly changing, though, with ideas expanding to match the potential of the students. Being flexible, searching for opportunities to adapt, and building on ideas are all a part of the school's philosophy.

The school counselor reinforces this idea of character education through classroom guidance work. Lavisi notes that building solid character goes hand-in-hand with building peer-pressure resistance skills, and the school begins early to teach both.

Building the classrooms around the community concept involves giving the kids some ownership of their environments and a strong sense of empowerment. Lavisi believes that if they can set some of their own rules, kids quickly understand the importance of responsibility and cooperation. Developing close relationships between teachers and children is also an important part of the program, and teachers feel that one of the most important parts of their jobs is to instill a sense of value in these children.

The children are granted increasing levels of responsibility as they mature and demonstrate the ability to manage their school activities. In turn, they respond by showing impressive capabilities to handle tasks normally reserved for adult administrators.

"If you go to an assembly program, you don't see me there taking charge," Lavisi says, "You'll see the counselor speak for about thirty seconds, then the kids take over. They run everything, the entire assembly program. They do our morning announcements, our afternoon announcements, they do all the special kinds of jobs that they can really do, but that adults generally have done."

Lavisi's innovative approach to education also includes strong ideas about the need for parental involvement and the connections between parents and adolescents. He feels that parents must be involved with character education and development to reinforce and support what their kids are learning in school.

"We are concerned about the trends that we're seeing with kids engaging in risky behavior," he explains, "We're redesigning our health education curriculum and introducing a very strong parent component in it. That's one part of the curriculum that must have parent involvement from the get-go.

"The more support you give kids, the more likely they are to be able to use refusal skills and wellness skills to lead a healthy lifestyle. You can't give up these kinds of curricular issues to outside agencies because once you do, it's a type of rationalization. You can say, 'Well, it's not our fault. That's their program, they messed up.' You have to take responsibility."

Teaching values and promoting character development may not fall into the traditional mold of "reading, writing, and arithmetic" as the most important basics for our educational system, but special times require special solutions. As a parent, you should consider not only the strength of this concept in the schools, but also its application in your home.

BUILDING RESPECT

If you understand and appreciate what your teenager is experiencing, if you know what your teenager is looking for and what's of concern to him, if you can relate to your teenager in ways that are interesting and important to him, you will build a basis of respect. Teenagers understand that there needs to be a degree of parental control, but as they explain it, they learn most when that control is occasionally relaxed. The teenagers of Generation Risk thrive on latitude and respect.

Anita

Anita is worried about her grades. She is meeting Amy tonight to study for a calculus test, but neither of them really understands the last chapter. Anita thinks calculus is so complicated and so stupid. But if she flunks this course, it will ruin her average. Anita is wearing a blue T-shirt, tan shorts, and Teva sandals with thick black soles and a patterned blue strap. Her toenails are painted light blue, and she has a small rose tattoo on her ankle.

"My dad lets you go out and do it on your own, but not too much. It's like a yo-yo. He's got the string on you, but he gives you a little bit of rope to let you make your own decisions. At the same time, if it's not for you, he won't let you do it and he'll tell you 'no,' and that's how you learn how to decide for yourself. Parents need to give their kids freedom so that when they tell us not to do something, we'll respect it more. We'll listen to them, and take their advice. Because if they tell us not to do everything, then we're not going to believe a word they say and we'll go out and try everything."

Teenagers are not reluctant to point out mistakes parents make when trying to communicate with them. These teenagers are open about their resentment and exasperation at normal parental interventions. They want more respect, more privacy, more trust, and more individual attention. They want you to appreciate their worlds and their individuality, and not just try to apply *your* experience to *their* problems. They want you to relate to them.

Tiffany

Tiffany has three younger sisters and lives with her mother, who works at night. At fifteen, Tiffany has a lot of responsibility. She cooks dinner most nights and looks after her sisters. She also argues with her mother a lot.

"Honestly, it ticks me off. My mom will not give anyone the same amount of respect she insists be given to her. Like if I'm on the phone trying to reach one of my friends, and I'm talking to someone's mom, she'll walk in and insist I talk to her right then."

In a recent *Nickelodeon/Time* poll of parents and children, the majority of parents claimed to have "a lot" of respect for kids, but the kids themselves thought that only 31 percent of adults respected them a lot. This "respect gap" was especially notable among kids twelve to fourteen (the oldest group in the survey), who said they get little or no respect from adults.

For teenagers who feel entitled to acknowledgment of their maturity and their accomplishments, a lack of respect is even more stinging.

Kim

Kim is cold, so she has pulled on a deep red sweater over her other clothes. She is tired, and she needs to get some sleep. She was out late last night with her friends.

"My mom always looks at the situation as, 'I'm the parent. I'm the boss of you.' I think she needs to look at the situation and in some cases, it needs to be like that, but mostly it should be like, 'We're both humans and treat me the same.' It's the same with people at my school. A lot of them are disrespectful to teachers. They're very disrespectful to teachers and higher authority—talking back, using profanity, and even saying really obscene things. To me it doesn't matter who it is, you need to show respect."

Negotiating with Generation Risk

One way to bridge the "respect gap" between you and your Generation Risk teenager is to negotiate some agreements. If you discuss areas of conflict and clarify what each of you wants to accomplish, you will often find common ground, and you will build respect.

And for any issue you raise with your teenager, you also need to explain your perspective.

Gary

Gary is of Cuban descent, with short dark hair and brown eyes. He is wearing tight jeans, cowboy boots, and a Hawaiian-print shirt that shows his chest hair. At sixteen, he listens to country music, but only to male singers. He doesn't like female country artists. He is holding his key ring by the red-and-black plastic attachment, a one-inch square drawing of a large red tongue with "Rolling Stones" in black script.

"Parents need to explain the 'why' about things. If they just say, 'Because I said so,' you disregard it and get mad. It's just so open and shut. That's it. Parents should treat teenagers not as though they're still children, but as though they can make intelligent choices. Give them all sides of the argument, and let them help figure it out."

As these teenagers gain maturity, they desperately want to be respected and to make their own decisions. To stay involved on important issues, parents have to be willing to negotiate with Generation Risk about which rules can be relaxed, which can be eliminated, and which ones are absolute.

A crucial point to remember about successful negotiations is that negotiating is not the same as compromising. You don't necessarily have to give up things that are important to you and end up with less than you want in order to reach agreement with your teenager.

The next point is that in order for *you* to win, *your teenager* doesn't necessarily have to lose. A good negotiation is one in which both parties win, and there are feelings of satisfaction all around. This idea is especially important to apply to conflicts with teenagers. If parents always dominate in negotiations, teenagers will probably resent and avoid the experience.

Here are some of the basic rules of successful negotiations that can help you resolve problems with your teenager:

Always allow your teenager to save face.

Being humiliated is a degrading, painful experience that creates hostility and erodes a person's sense of self-worth. Allow your teenager to make concessions while preserving his sense of dignity.

Be willing to give up some things.

This strategy goes hand-in-hand with saving face. Your teenager has to gain something in order to feel that the effort is worthwhile.

Know ahead of time which things are absolute "must-haves" from your perspective.

If you understand which things are critical to you, you can explain them up front. Then you can focus on areas of give-and-take.

Work to find common ground early in the discussion.

By establishing a shared goal, you can create a stronger incentive on both sides to work out differences. By enumerating areas of agreement, you will minimize the weight of the problems to be resolved. You will end up working together against the problem instead of working against each other.

Resist the temptation to repeat your own arguments.

Make your point once, then move on. Going in circles just creates frustration and ultimately gives everybody a headache. If you only repeat your positions without changing them, you appear to be stubborn and a poor listener.

Listen to your teenager's point of view carefully, and understand her absolute "must-haves" so that you can try to accommodate them.

If you recognize the areas that are out of bounds, you can avoid forcing the discussion into a deadlock. If one solution doesn't work for both of you, maybe another will. If you both really want to solve the problem, you can accommodate each other's "must-haves." Try unconventional approaches to resolve the remaining items.

Work together to find solutions.

If you and your teenager both feel the agreement is at least partially your idea, you will feel a pride of authorship and will be more likely to support the decision later.

Working Together: How Late Is Late Enough?

Let's think of an example—say, setting a curfew—an issue around which there are frequently major disputes in families. Our son Ted recently asked that his curfew be extended from midnight on weekend nights to 12:30 A.M. My husband and I felt that midnight was late enough for Ted to be out unless some special event, such as a high school prom, was involved. After all, we reasoned, what more fun could he have in another thirty minutes compared to the first six or seven hours of the evening? (Ted has cleverly increased his "going out" time over the last couple of years by gradually easing the beginning of the evening forward.)

Without consciously setting out to do so, we entered into a negotiation about the subject. The first step was to understand exactly what our son was seeking, and why. Was it the extra half-hour? Was it more freedom? Did it have something to do with peer pressure? Did he want a reward for abiding pretty well by the previous curfew?

Once we listened to his reasons, we understood that he wanted recognition for the fact that he was seventeen years old and felt that he should be given more responsibility in line with his level of maturity. Then we expressed our concerns. We don't sleep soundly (or at all) when our kids are out. We worry about drunk drivers late at night. We worry about what our boy will be involved in after the movies are long over and local parties extend into the night.

We thought about a compromise of 12:15 A.M. But this "solution" really wouldn't have made any of us happy. As parents, we would be giving in to something we felt was unnecessary and slightly dangerous. As a teenager whose peers had later curfews than his own, Ted would be denied the trust to which he felt entitled (and perhaps would have wished that he had simply asked for a 1:00 A.M. curfew so we would have compromised on 12:30 A.M.).

Our negotiations proceeded to stage two. We sought "common ground." We told Ted that we had been really pleased with the maturity he had demonstrated by coming home on time or calling to explain any unforeseen delays. We complimented him on his driving record, on his reliability in feeding the dog when we left him in charge of her, and on his haircut. We acknowledged that he has been a "good citizen." We told him that we agreed he should be given some more freedom, not merely because he was seventeen, but because he was acting responsibly. Then we explained that this particular form of freedom was not something we felt good about.

The "common ground" was recognition of Ted's increased maturity. Once we acknowledged that we appreciated his behavior, Ted seemed satisfied that his objective had actually been achieved. It turned out he didn't really care about the extra half-hour and that if it bothered us, he didn't really need to stay out later.

We reminded Ted that just the week before, we had given him permission to spend his spring break week visiting his sister at her college campus, and that by doing so we were showing that we trusted his judgment. Even though he didn't get what he had asked for, our teenage son came through this "negotiation" a winner. We articulated our feelings in a way that made him feel proud of himself, and he agreed with our decision.

Another way to build respect is to make contracts with your teenager.

Contracts and Other Promises

Businesses use contracts to make sure that everybody settles the details of deals. When you sign a contract, you feel committed because you've formalized an agreement. Before you sign a contract, you should think about what you're getting into and what you're getting out of it.

Contracts written by lawyers often have terminology the rest of us find difficult to understand, and even the simplest of intentions can become caught up in "hereins," "parties of the first part," "notwithstandings," and "whereas" recitations. But everybody makes contracts when we make agreements with each other, including families. Contracts don't have to be complicated. By following a few solid business practices and writing down the terms of the pacts you make with your children, you can gain mutual respect.

Reaching agreement on a contract is a give-and-take process, a negotiation that reaches a firm conclusion. Negotiations only work well when both sides are balanced like a seesaw on a playground. A good contract makes both parties feel that the deal is fair, that they each get something they want, and that nobody is left stranded in mid-air with legs flailing helplessly while the other side sits dominantly on the ground.

You can make use of contracts to help clarify the rules for your teenager. When kids have literally "signed up" not to smoke, drink, or use illegal drugs, they not only understand the consequences of breaking the contract and the rewards of abiding by it, but they also have a tool to use in resisting peer pressure. They can cite the existence of the contract (and the associated penalties if it is broken) as a concrete way of warding off temptations.

To be effective, a good contract doesn't have to be written down and signed, but it should be well thought out. You have an opportunity to make deals with your kids every day. For example, you might allow a teenage son to borrow the car if he cuts the grass and promises to drive carefully. You might give a teenage daughter permission to have a party for her friends if she agrees to clean up afterwards and keep things under control.

These deals are more powerful if you take the time to spell out consequences in case something goes wrong, if you make sure the rewards are worth the effort, and if you both understand the scope of the agreement:

How large a party, and how late into the night will it last? What action do you expect your teenager to take if somebody shows up with beer or liquor? How much privacy will you allow as responsible parents? How loud may the music be played?

The best contracts have these characteristics:

- **Clarity:** The contract should be understandable, not so clouded with formal language that an interpreter is required.
- **Balance:** it should be fair to both parties involved, not lopsidedly in favor of one or the other.
- **Completeness:** It should cover all the possibilities, not just the most likely things to happen.
- **Value:** It should be of benefit to both parties, so they want to sign instead of feel they have to sign.

These principles are logical, common sense ideas you can apply in the cold light of day and that should stand up in the dark hours of the night when teenagers often need something concrete to rely on.

Yet as methodical and logical as you might try to be, you are dealing with people, not machines. Your teenagers are often driven more by emotion than logic. Achieving balance in a contract requires establishing the right mix of control versus flexibility, involvement versus freedom, and protectiveness versus opportunity for your teenager.

You also have to expect some mistakes.

DID YOU LEARN ANYTHING?

As a college professor, my husband has had lots of experience dealing with teenagers in freshman survey classes. His tolerance for what he describes as "air-heads" is fairly low, and his approach to teaching is very individual. He has often challenged his students to think about the significance of things they have observed or experienced or read—not a skill that comes easily to many young people.

One vivid example of his approach to teenagers occurred on a rainy afternoon in Indiana when he was out in his workshop. He heard the unmistakable sounds of skidding tires, then the grinding of metal and glass and bricks as a teenager, driving too fast on our curvy, hilly road, came crashing into one of our maple trees. The car careened into and obliterated one of the brick pillars beside our driveway. My husband threw open the door of our garage and rushed outside as several teenage boys were climbing out of their demolished Camero, dazed but clearly unharmed. Instead of asking the expected question about whether they were okay, my husband opened with the brusque (and timely) question, "Did you *learn* anything?"

The boys were startled into thinking not only about what had happened, but why. By the time a parent arrived (and the boys had recovered their composure at our kitchen table), their lesson for the day was firmly embedded. They would not speed on our street again, and perhaps would think carefully about driving conditions in rainy weather ever after.

As parents who care about teaching your teenagers to think for themselves, you can apply something from this example, too. When your teenagers make mistakes, *involve them in analyzing why* so they can be armed with information and so they will resolve to avoid the problem in the future.

If your kids are hurt, they need care and sometimes cuddling. If they misbehave, they need discipline. If they make mistakes, they need to learn something from them. Sometimes, they need all three.

HOW MUCH IS ENOUGH?

As a parent, you're trapped in a tough situation. If you try to act like a friend to your teenager instead of a disciplinarian, he might not respect you or your authority. You may inadvertently be shirking your responsibilities to provide appropriate structure and boundaries. On the other horn of the dilemma, if you set firm rules, then you risk being too strict or overprotective. A lot of teenagers complain that their parents constantly pick on them, mistrust them, or lecture them.

Anita

Anita has kicked off her sandals and is sitting on her left foot. She is irritated that she is missing her favorite program on MTV, and she wants to get out of this interview.

"I wish my parents would realize that I'm not going to be like other bad people. I know they love me, but they don't trust me. I'm like, 'Leave me alone.' It doesn't get through to them. I have this friend, her parents are really overprotective. All her mom does instead of being open and talking to her is threaten her and say 'no.' So she is out of control. One day my friend is going to bust out of her shell and go buck wild. If your parents hold you back, it's like a bulldog on a chain. Eventually they'll break the chain and go crazy."

You need to demonstrate that you trust your teenager. Part of the motivation for Generation Risk to rebel comes from the lack of responsibility they feel for their own actions. If parents trust and depend on them to act responsibly, then they feel an obligation to pay attention.

Latelle

Latelle is wearing straw-colored platform shoes that she just bought at the mall. Her hair is braided and tied with small gold ribbons at the end of each section, and she is wearing a long-sleeved, creamy-white sweater and brown stretch pants. Beside her is a handled shopping bag with the tan suede jacket she found on sale at her favorite store.

"My mother is after me about everything. She fusses about the phone, about my room, my clothes. Oooooh. Whoever I hang out with. She fusses about everything. We scream, yell, throw fits, get dramatic. I couldn't care less, really, because I mean she's too overprotective. I ignore her."

You need to strike an appropriate balance, to discharge your responsibilities as a parent without suffocating your teenager in the process. You can't withdraw from this challenge.

VALUES, AND OTHER PEOPLE'S CHILDREN

I sometimes work with a business ethics professor at the University of Virginia. He endures a lot of kidding about his subject: "Business ethics? Ha. Ha. Must be a short course." In reality, this subject is far from humorous. It is central to business success, because each of us must apply our personal values to our work environment in order to build trust with each other and with our customers.

In the same way, values make up the innermost core of your relationship with your teenager and form the basis of the trust you share. You have to decide which values are critical to nurture in your teenager to help him withstand the pressures that are all around.

To help you focus on the few most vital issues with your teenager, one approach is to think about the most important values *you wish other people would instill in their children.* Deciding on core values is not so difficult a task. You want your teenager to do the right thing, to be honest, to respect himself and others, to have integrity, and to be trustworthy. If you can teach the basics, the rest will flow from these few central values.

But how do you teach integrity? How do you instill a sense of respect in your kids? These are tough questions, and many parents struggle to answer them. The best recourse is to be role models for your kids and to display the values you want them to develop.

One of my friends was recently discussing his martial arts lessons. He overheard another parent asking the instructor about the availability of lessons for teenagers because his son needed to learn some discipline. The instructor replied wisely, "I can enroll you in a class for adults on Wednesdays."

It's up to parents to provide the example. You can't expect to buy discipline lessons for your teenagers, and you can't buy them values.

TRUST: A CURRENCY WORTH ITS WEIGHT IN GOLD

Teens who feel close to their parents talk about trust. In almost every case, they still engage in some form of risk-taking, but often the degree of risk-taking is more controlled among teenagers who speak of parental involvement.

Albert

Albert is chewing on the tip of his pen and thinking about the lyrics from his new Dave Matthews Band CD. Albert is wearing a Bart Simpson T-shirt and jean shorts. His backpack is on the floor beside him, filled with school books.

"I'm really open with my mom and dad. They're understanding. They're really smart. They tell me, 'That was a bad decision. You shouldn't do that again.' I'm never gonna do drugs again. I feel like I can talk to my parents, but a lot of kids don't. You have to be open with your parents. I might not feel like saying stuff, but I do anyway. With me, trust isn't something you have. It's something you have to earn with your parents."

Many teenagers use trust as an anchor. In the age of Generation Risk, teenagers need stability and motivation to avoid dangers. Don't underestimate the influence you have on your teenager. It's the *absence of parental involvement* that drives many teenagers to take thoughtless risks.

Marie

Marie has a part-time job at a Mexican restaurant near her house. She has worked there for three years and is allowed to wait tables, but not to serve liquor because she is only sixteen. She is wearing jeans and her red uniform shirt that says Tumbleweed on front and The Best Tacos in Town on the back.

"My momma has helped me with relationships. She always wants me to tell her my problems with what's going on in relationships. We just talk about it. She lets me do things because we have trust with each other, and that's why I don't lie to her."

Teenagers understand that trust must be earned and that it can be lost in a careless second. They seem inclined to work for trust if they feel it will be fairly granted because it is such a valued commodity.

Tamara

Tamara is leaning forward with her elbows on the table and her face in her hands. She is thinking about what Marie just said. She is tapping her right foot.

"My mom always said that if we build up her trust, she'll give us a little bit of freedom each year. She gives us more, and then when you just do

something to take her trust away, then you have to start over to build that trust back up. As long as I keep that trust built, I get more freedom and independence every day."

Teenagers believe in each other. Their mutual trust is one of the sources of the power of the peer group. Parents can bond with their teenagers through trust as well.

Marie

Marie never wants to see another taco. She is sick of being around Mexican food and sick of waiting on tables. But she has to go to work in an hour. She needs to earn money to pay for her clothes.

"I think since teenagers want to be adults so bad, I think you should try to treat them like adults. Like give them the benefit of the doubt and trust them until they prove themselves wrong. I find that friends with parents who have trust in them, they'll continue to be good because they're like, 'I don't want to lose that trust.' So you should give them a chance."

Teenagers depend on their peers about matters of music and clothing, but they give parental opinions more weight on the important issues of vocational choices, morals, and social values. In studies of situations in which conflicting advice is offered by peers versus parents, teenagers do not typically acquiesce to peer pressure and they rely on their own judgment more than either peers or adults providing advice.

You have a special opportunity as a parent to influence your teenager. Generation Risk needs discipline, responsibility, and trust. Your teenager needs a strong sense of values to guide his independent decision-making. But you also need to keep tabs on his self-esteem.

BUILDING YOUR TEENAGER'S SELF-ESTEEM

Decades of research provides compelling evidence that there are three factors at the root of most teenage problems: *self-esteem, self-esteem,* and *self-esteem.*

Tennis star Andre Agassi struck at the core of the teenage psyche when he proclaimed in a camera commercial a few years ago, "Image is everything." Far from being a shallow veneer, self-image permeates the psychological fiber of teenagers and affects their attitudes, behaviors, capabilities, and character.

Self-esteem has a huge impact on performance that stems from childhood. Several studies conducted by various research groups reveal that if kids feel good about themselves, they make better grades in school, all the way from the primary grades through their undergraduate years. Self-confidence breeds success. Achievement in school is directly proportionate to self-esteem.

The implications of these findings are incredibly powerful and far-reaching. Success in school has a direct bearing on future earning power, career options, and ability to attain self-sufficiency. Self-esteem is the premium fuel that drives human performance.

The relationship between self-esteem and performance is especially significant to parents of teenagers, because the Surgeon General reports a direct connection between performance in school and smoking. *If your teenager has higher self-esteem, there's a better chance that he will not smoke. If your teenager likes school and has expectations of school success, there's a better chance that he will not smoke.*

There's also a powerful correlation between juvenile delinquency and low self-esteem, and cumulative studies have demonstrated that low self-esteem is a contributor to high rates of teen pregnancy. A plethora of research provides indisputable evidence that boosting self-esteem is a positive strategy for protecting teenagers from risks.

Almost every study that identifies root causes of teenage problems leads back to self-esteem. The formation of gangs is connected to the need for recognition, a sense of belonging, and tradition—all related to self-esteem. In a society of single-parent households, high-stress living, and dehumanizing computer interfaces, we have a special opportunity and an inherent obligation to fulfill these esteem-building needs for our teenagers through personal interaction at home.

The list goes on and on. Low self-esteem is pegged as a causal factor in neurosis, anxiety, defensiveness, and, ultimately, alcohol and drug use. Clinical studies have documented the relationship of low self-esteem in adolescents to depression and thoughts of suicide. What could be more threatening or more important?

The message to parents is clear. *We need to build self-esteem in our teenagers, and the more the better.* Even when problems already exist, research proves that school programs designed to increase self-esteem can significantly change the attitudes of students about alcohol and drug use.

Parents can do even more.

How to Nurture Self-Esteem

How can parents help? *In dozens of ways.* No one cares more about our teenagers or has more ability to influence their self-esteem than we do. We can cultivate self-esteem in our children by providing a positive environment. We can praise our children for their qualities and accomplishments, teach them skills that enhance their ability to perform, and encourage them to expand their horizons. When we discipline our kids, we can be careful not to attack their feelings of self-worth but to address their *behavior* instead. We can fortify their emotional growth by instilling strong values. We can build bonds of trust and *empower them to make decisions on their own.*

A good starting point for building self-esteem is the development of sound social skills. Adolescents and teenagers want nothing more than to be accepted by their friends, to fit in with the group. Their desire to belong drives conformity to styles of dress, taste in music, haircuts, and use of language. To be different is to be wrong, and to be rejected is devastating.

Strengthening skills that can promote their popularity and acceptance among their peers is certain to help teenagers feel better about themselves. If they feel comfortable in social situations and have the skills to forge new friendships, their self-esteem will blossom.

How to Carry on a Conversation

Many teenagers don't have *any* conversational skills, and this deficiency can get them into trouble. Whether talking to a peer or an adult, a teen who lacks the ability to communicate easily or express himself feels ill at ease, which immediately erodes self-esteem. No matter how "cool" a teen felt coming into school or arriving at a party, it is difficult to feel good about himself, if he is left not knowing what to say.

A typical conversation between teenagers who don't know each other well might be as follows:

Justin: *Hey, man. What's going on?*
Matt: *Nuthin', man.*

These teenagers are *breaking the ice.* But with no conversational skills to maintain their comfort level, they could feel compelled to relieve the pressure of an awkward silence by reaching for the nearest risk. For example, one teenager could offer the other a cigarette.

Justin: *Wanna smoke?*
Matt: *Sure.*

Now they are *bonding,* but not in a positive way. They are both engaging in a risky behavior when really all they want to do is to get to know each other better.

We can teach our teenagers the secrets of starting a good conversation that will help them bypass the need for cigarettes or alcohol or drugs as props. The first step is to figure out the other person's goals, interests, involvements, or accomplishments. The next step is to use our own experience or knowledge on these topics to build up the conversation. It's important that both partners contribute, so that nobody dominates. A good analogy is a jam session in jazz, which starts with conventional elements, but builds into an exciting new composition as contributors add spontaneous variations.

Armed with good conversation skills, teenagers have an expanded array of positive options for engaging each other.

> Justin: *Nice shirt, man.* (Matt is wearing a T-shirt from a Smashing Pumpkins rock concert.) *Have you heard their new single?*

Now they've established a *common interest* and a platform for social interaction based on words, not risk.

Conversational dexterity can help teenagers parry the thrusts of temptation and expand their vistas of friendship. A wonderful technique to help kids learn conversation skills is to compare a good conversation to tennis. We can explain that the idea in tennis is to keep hitting the ball back. In conversation, when one person talks, that's hitting the ball over the net.

When the ball comes to you on your side of the net, you hit it back. You don't let it fly past you without reacting. In conversation, you don't just let comments float past without responding. You listen to what was said, then make a comment of your own. That's hitting the ball back across the net.

Conversation doesn't have to be devastatingly clever, just as every shot in tennis doesn't have to be a winning stroke. You just hit the ball with your racket, aiming it where you want it to go, and return it to the other side of the net. That's acknowledging what the other person had to say, and maybe adding a reaction or asking a related question.

You have to exert effort to swing at the tennis ball to keep the point alive, just as you have to work at keeping a conversation flowing. But once you begin, the exchange becomes natural, and when you practice your game, your technique improves.

If teenagers have good conversational skills, they will have a much better chance of *talking their way* through social situations and resisting the insidious pressures they will face during their teenage years.

Practicing conversation skills at home with our teenagers can reap huge rewards. If our teenagers are comfortable with conversation, and if we keep up a running dialogue, they are more likely to *come to us about important topics*.

Content of practice sessions doesn't really matter. We can talk about sports or about our family pets. In fact, the less personal the better at the outset, just to increase our teenager's comfort level. What is important is that the words keep flowing, that our kids become engaged in the process, and that they exercise their minds in the direction of making conversation.

The more we talk to our teenagers about anything at all, the better we will know them, and the more comfortable we will be in trusting their judgment and maturity.

Expectations and Empowerment

In a lot of families, parents don't expect much from their teenagers. They assume their teenagers will lie around sleeping or sit around watching television all weekend unless forced to perform some required chores. Parents who rely on power to define their roles tend to be critical and to use their authority to enforce rules and stimulate action.

Another way of dealing with teenagers is to create a more positive, empowering climate, which allows a lot more latitude. In families where children are encouraged to be more independent, are trusted with more information, and participate in solving problems, kids take more responsibility or "ownership" for their actions. Using this "empowerment" approach, parents share more information, encourage initiative, and treat teenagers as sources of ideas. Kids in this environment are expected to take some risks, and occasional mistakes are tolerated as part of the process.

At the heart of an empowerment climate is trust. If you give teenagers a chance to perform, they probably will. But the more rigid you are, the more you create resistance. The more you demand, the more they have to resist.

When teenagers talk about their feelings, they confirm this theory about the balance of power between their parents and themselves. They say that if we exert too much control over them, we can provoke a rebellious backlash. Teenagers reveal intense feelings when they talk about their emotional reactions to excessive parental control because power is a currency that kids don't have. When they feel they're on the short end of the power stick, they misbehave to even up the score.

Aaron

Aaron is wearing jeans, a T-shirt, and a plaid shirt untucked and open in front. His shoes are oversized brown monsters with thick soles that add about two inches to his height. His hands are jammed into his front pockets and his head is cocked to the side. He is scowling. At age fifteen, Aaron is ready for some freedom. He seems to have constant conflicts with his parents who order him to do chores, limit his curfew to unreasonable hours, and make him beg for permission just to spend the night out at a friend's house.

"My parents like to remind me that they have power and I don't. They're constantly telling me what to do. It makes me want to do something to break away. If kids are being held down so long, so much all the time, or being ordered to do things for so long, they have to do something or they're going to burst inside."

Pent-up frustration can ignite an explosion of rebellion within volatile and emotional teenagers. Their submission to authority may only represent the deceptive dormant stage that precedes a volcanic eruption. Trust and empowerment provide escape valves for pressurized steam that diffuse the potentially explosive forces of frustration and anger in our teenagers and build their self-esteem. Coaching can help as well.

Coaching to Build Confidence

Coaches excel at developing strategy and tactics, and, in the same sense that's the role we can play as parents. We want our children to be successful, and as long as they understand the goal and the game plan, there's a good chance they'll accept our guidance.

If we are effective at coaching, our players (our children) will want to employ the strategies and skills we've helped to develop in them. Just as a coach doesn't go into the game with his players, parents don't accompany their children through their various contests with temptations and challenges. Our role is to teach the basics, to strengthen skills, then to watch from the bench and be ready to help celebrate victories or recover from losses.

The more confident our teenagers are about their own judgment, the better equipped they will be to resist simply going along with the crowd. But coaching is not an automatic activity to parents, especially when we are used to the role of disciplinarian or teacher.

A good coaching example is the process of teaching a child to ride a bicycle. It doesn't help a lot to talk about theory or to provide a series of warnings about what might go wrong. It also doesn't help to demonstrate excessively by riding around the yard pointing out biking tips. The more we instruct by pointing to ourselves in this particular exercise, the more frustrated and impatient the child will become. Finally, we have to expect a few falls. We can run alongside the bicycle only so far and so long, then we have to give a shove and let go. The role of the teacher and authority figure then transforms to the role of coach. We give advice, then we help pick up the child, dust off the dirt, praise progress, and support another attempt. The main thing we can do to help is *to encourage him to try it for himself.*

As parents, we need to be willing to throw our kids into the water sometimes and let them learn to swim. We need to encourage them to try new experiences and to be ready to rescue them if they sink. By showing that we want them to develop new skills and expand their horizons, we can build their self-esteem and self-confidence in a safe but not overprotective environment.

Accomplishment builds self-esteem. Teenagers can even derive a sense of pride from involvement in activities they initially resist if they accomplish *something that is significant to them.* They can have a much greater extent of control if they measure themselves by what they have done instead of how they look or what they own.

We have to expect a few skinned knees as our kids grow through their teenage years. We're not perfect, and we shouldn't expect them to be, either. This doesn't mean we should encourage our teenagers to try dangerous things for themselves or that we should accept whatever they do. We need to establish boundaries for their behavior, to explain the rules and the reasons for the rules, and to enforce them. When our kids make mistakes or break the rules, one of our most important roles is to help them *learn from their own mistakes*, since they have a tougher time learning from ours.

Feedback that Builds Self-Esteem

Everybody gives feedback, and quite a lot of it. Feedback can be visual, verbal, or tactile. It can be blatant or subtle, polite or rude. It can be constructive or devastating. In fact, feedback is such a powerful tool and is so often poorly used, that it typically fills many hours in management training programs.

If we want to be effective at giving feedback to our teenagers instead of striking nerves, we can make use of some proven techniques. One idea that works is to give some positive feedback first, slip in a constructive comment, and then complete the "sandwich" with something complimentary.

For example, imagine that your teenage daughter Anita has just cooked hamburgers for the two of you. You might be tempted to say, "*Oh, honey. That's too much onion for me.*" Even though your comment might be intended as an innocent remark, it could be interpreted by a sensitive teenager as a criticism. An alternative approach, using the "sandwich" technique would be to start off by saying, "*Oh, honey. This hamburger is just delicious.*" This remark builds confidence and establishes a basis of positive feelings. Next you could add, "*I think I could do with a little less onion.*" This comment is not a compliment to Anita, but it is mitigated by the compliment that preceded it. Finally, you could complete the exchange by adding, "*You know, I really think you are a great cook.*" The overall impact of this feedback is positive and the message about drowning the hamburger in onion is still conveyed, but without hurting Anita's feelings or damaging her self-esteem.

Another suggestion is to be specific rather than general. Specific feedback might be, "*Heather, you repeated the word 'cool' five times in the second paragraph of your paper. How about finding a synonym or rephrasing to provide some variety for the reader?*" This technique would be more helpful than saying, "*Heather, you always say the same thing over and over.*" General feedback is more difficult to address because it is vague.

Effective feedback also focuses on the actions or behavior, not on the person. "*Matthew, I am angry because you wrecked my car*" addresses behavior. "*Matthew, you idiot, you are the worst driver I have ever seen*" is critical of the person. We shouldn't be personal when we give feedback to other people, especially our teenagers. They are incredibly sensitive, and they remember the painful things we say long after we forget them.

Accentuating the Positive

Effective feedback doesn't have to come in the form of constructive criticism. It can also be *purely positive.* As parents, we never seem to forget to deliver negative feedback, but it's easy to overlook the chances to give positive feedback. "*Thanks for coming home on time*" is probably heard a lot less often by the teenagers of America than "*You were late last night.*"

A business example can help illustrate the value of emphasizing positives. In business we often use brainstorming as a way of generating creative ideas. This process involves tossing out lots of ideas to encourage each other's creativity. One of the most important rules of brainstorming is not to reject any ideas in the early stages, no matter how ridiculous they might seem. The reason is that *criticism stifles creativity.* Many ideas grow from each other, and even a silly seed of a thought, if allowed to live, can flourish later when it is transformed and built upon by positive thinkers. But even as adults, when our ideas are dismissed, our self-esteem suffers and our participation tends to shut down.

When we talk to our teenagers about their behavior, we should remember the value of being positive. Regardless of what mistakes they may have made, we can find something positive in the experience—even if it's only to contrast it with what might have been worse. Putting teenage transgressions into context may try our patience, but it will also soften our urge to criticize too harshly. If we build on positives, we have a better chance of being heard.

As parents who have provided feedback, guidance, and discipline to our children during their whole lives, it may be difficult for us to understand that our teenagers have suddenly become super-sensitive to any form of suggestion for change, which they interpret as criticism. It never feels good to be criticized. We can sometimes swallow constructive feedback in the way we tolerate an insipid dose of medicine, but we never savor it.

Being criticized is like taking a round of body punches. Once, when the famous heavyweight boxing champion Joe Louis was interviewed after a fight, the announcer said something like, "*Joe, your opponent didn't seem to like those body punches.*" The Champ sagely replied, "*Who do?*"

Teenagers may be even more sensitive to criticism than the rest of us. The typical teenager is like a porcupine with nerve endings exposed like quills. If we are critical of our teens, we are likely to hit a nerve and inflict pain. In turn, they will shoot back quills in the form of rebellion.

Being a Cheerleader

When sports teams play home fields, they usually have a better chance of winning than when they are on the road. There's something about having their fans cheering for them and providing support, something about the familiarity of their environment, something about the security of belonging, that gives the home team an edge. In a similar way, our kids have an advantage trying to compete against the pressures they face if they can do it on their home turf, with the support and cheering of their families to help them win. We have a chance to be our kids' biggest fans.

Being a cheerleader for our teenagers is different from simply giving good feedback. Good cheerleading is an expression of confidence, encouragement, and loyalty. "The Tigers are the best" conveys a message to the team that the fans believe in them. This message works in concert with "All for the Tigers stand up and holler," which is also important, because it says that the fans are behind the team, supporting the efforts of the players. A third kind of cheer is to implore the team to exert itself, "Block that kick!"

The three messages to teenagers that cheerleading can establish are the following:

• I'm on your side—no matter what.
• I think you're terrific.
• Go for it. You can achieve anything.

A few years ago, I was fortunate enough to spend a day with the well-known management consultant, Peter Drucker, discussing business topics that ranged from leadership to empowerment. Dr. Drucker believes that the *greatest development experience for any person* is achievement. He advises us to be sure to point out to people what their *strengths* are, not just their weaknesses.

The importance of giving this kind of recognition cannot be overemphasized. The more we make our teenagers aware of their strengths, the better they will feel about themselves. The more we build their confidence to take responsibility for their own decisions, the more thoughtful those decisions are likely to be.

LATITUDE AND ATTITUDE

We must also recognize that our teenagers need a certain amount of latitude to evolve into their roles as responsible adults. They may even deserve an occasional opportunity to behave irrationally.

My friend Linda has a daughter who is thirteen, and ready to express her independence by coloring her hair. Apparently she's a pretty savvy kid, because she asked for parental permission, and has actually established some ground rules up front.

Linda was pleased to be consulted in advance, and wanted to be as supportive a parent as possible. She suggested a reasonable plan, "You have permission to color your hair, but if it looks terrible, then we'll have it professionally redone."

In turn, her daughter got immediately to the heart of the matter by asking, "Well, what if I think it looks good, and you think it looks terrible?"

After some careful consideration, Linda decided that whatever the outcome of the hair, the outcome of the interaction between parent and child was more important. She resolved not to criticize her daughter's hair, no matter how outlandish, realizing that arguing would only make her daughter dig in her heels.

Teenagers feel they have to experience certain things for themselves, that they have to rebel at least slightly just to establish a sense of individuality and independence.

More than any other factor, the attainment of a healthy sense of identity gives young people the ability to manage stressful situations. If they have self-esteem, they tend to look at situations from the other person's perspective as well as their own, and this process gives them a balanced view and an ability to cope.

Camille

Camille has just shaved her head. Her head has a lovely shape, and her hair is not really completely shaved, just sheared off very close to the scalp. She has piercing black eyes and long, curly lashes. Camille has never gone along with the crowd in the sense that most teenagers conform to the standards of their peer group. At seventeen, she's just as unconventional and unpredictable as she has ever been—and just as determined to prove that she's capable of making her own decisions.

"I know there are a lot of bad things in the world, and we have to sample a few of them. But just because you've tasted something, that doesn't mean you're going to eat the whole dish. I think there's a certain point where you have to break away. Then once you establish yourself, you can still look back at your parents and agree with some things. It's just that, you've got to do it on your own. Sometimes you just do things because you think your parents are making too many decisions for you. You just want to make some of your own decisions to feel a little bit more confident."

Giving our kids some latitude on small matters can pay off later. When we take a strong stand on really important issues, they'll understand the difference. In the meantime, they'll develop the self-confidence to handle many problems on their own.

PART III

HOW TO PREVENT SMOKING

10

DON'T
SAY DON'T

If you really want your teenager *not to do something*, about the worst thing you can say is, "*Don't do that.*" For teenagers, being restricted by parents is about as enjoyable as missing the best party of the year, washing dishes, or doing homework. Teenagers dislike being told "don't." Parents know it. Kids know it. Yet we still seem to use this technique as the primary form of communicating the rules to our teenagers.

Teenagers think of the word "don't" as a challenge to rebel. Their reactions to "don't" range from resentment to frustration to determination, and are almost always negative. For the teenagers of Generation Risk who are used to unprecedented freedoms, singling out certain behaviors with the label "don't" is like painting them with iridescent colors: forbidden activities glow in the dark like signposts attracting teenagers to rebel against parental authority.

LIKE WAVING A RED FLAG IN FRONT OF A BULL

In early 1998, as part of a youth smoking prevention program, I was involved in some focus group research among parents and teenagers to try to develop effective ways of communicating a message to kids to discourage them from smoking. We amassed a wide range of colorful, engaging logos that were intended to provide pizzazz, spark, involvement, and other desirable characteristics to appeal to the teenage audience. With each logo was a companion "tag line" such as *"Don't Start Smoking," "Don't Smoke Under 18," "Don't Smoke,"* or *"Be Smoke Free."*

What we learned from this research was enlightening and unequivocal. It was *unanimously* agreed among older teenage boys, younger teenage boys, older teenage girls, younger teenage girls—everybody—that using the word "*don't*" would be a big mistake.

Teenagers display emotionally charged reactions to being told "don't." Many consider this word not so much a warning as a challenge or a dare. They want to disprove and defy adults by ignoring their advice.

Patricia

Patricia is sitting at the table with her legs stretched out in front of her, back straight, her body forming almost a straight line from head to toe. Patricia is on the soccer team, and she is dressed in a green warmup suit and white T-shirt with her school logo emblazoned on the back. There is a white stripe down the side of the pants with the word "Cougars" in green script.

"Of course we dislike the word 'don't.' Who's saying it? What gives them the right to control your life? I mean, just hearing that word kind of makes you want to defy it. I resent it, because I think I'm old enough now to figure out what to do and what not to do on my own. It's too bossy to just give you this list of what not to do, like you aren't capable of making your own judgments. People will do things if you say 'don't' just because someone said not to."

Many kids think the word "don't" is so overused that it's simply ineffectual. They tune out parents and concentrate on something else when this sort of negative advice is showered on them. The teenagers of Generation Risk are used to dealing with multiple concurrent stimuli and focusing on just the parts that interest them. They are experienced at watching music videos while talking on the phone, writing e-mails while listening to their CD players, and watching television while doing homework. Blocking out parental advice is easy, especially when it's signaled by the red-flag word "don't."

Tamara

Tamara is eating a Subway sandwich and drinking a bottle of Fruitopia punch. Her earrings are thick silver half-moons, and she has a single zircon stud about an inch above the earring on her right ear. She is wearing a braided silver ring on her left thumb. Tamara is a junior.

"It's just a command. Kids get tired of people telling us what to do. That's a word I hear at least a thousand times a day. 'Don't go outside. Don't do drugs. Don't, don't, don't, don't, don't.' It doesn't even mean anything to me anymore. I've heard it so many times, I can't even remember."

You might as well be saying, "I dare you" to some kids when you say "don't." They consider it a challenge or a test of courage, will, or daring to defy the parents or teachers who are limiting their freedoms. Saying "don't" to rebellious teenagers offers them an opportunity to demonstrate their independence in specific ways that they know will be noticed.

Dean

Dean is relaxing and leaning back in his chair, thinking about calling the other guys so they can decide what to do tonight. His feet are crossed at the ankles, and his weight is resting on the heel of his right foot. His hands are folded together behind his head. Dean lives with his father. When his parents were divorced two years ago, his mother moved back to North Carolina. Dean was fifteen at the time and wanted to finish high school with his friends, so he stayed behind with his dad. He doesn't really like his father's new girlfriend, who is around the house a lot. But Dean doesn't spend that much time at home anyway. He'd rather be with his friends.

"It's what you're not allowed to do. Like, you go through your whole life wanting to get your driver's license. Then you get it and your mom says, 'Go get milk,' and you're like, 'I don't want to drive right now.' If you weren't allowed to drive, you'd jump at the chance. 'Don't' is like a challenge: 'How do I disobey my parents?' I think, 'You can't stop me.' Say there's like a wall. If somebody says, 'Don't go there,' you go anyway. It's like you're test-ing your own will by trying it. It makes me want to do that thing more. It tests you to do it."

Some teenagers almost seem to laugh at the word "don't," figuring that they can always find a way to do whatever they please. For other, less-defi-ant teens, being told "don't" simply frustrates them and makes them resent their parents. They may go along with a command, but not willingly. Instead of understanding *why not to do something*, and being armed with the emotional conviction to avoid whatever it is, these teens may simply be waiting for a chance to try another form of the forbidden behavior from which they haven't been specifically banned. They don't like being treated like children and feel they should be allowed to make their own decisions.

Jay

Jay is ready to head for the game as soon as the interview ends. He is dressed in a plaid shirt, gray T-shirt, and jeans with outer pockets that extend down almost to his knees. His pant legs cascade over the tops of his running shoes, sort of pooling around his ankles just like three of the other guys in the group. Jay's mother hates this new style of clothes, but he thinks it looks cool.

"When a parent says 'don't,' there's something that clicks in the teenager's mind that they're going to do it anyway. Like, 'I'm going to do it because I want to do it.' You can always find a way to get around the rules. You can find a loophole, or sort of hopscotch around them. When they just say 'don't,' it makes me want to do it even more, and I get frustrated. Like

if your mom doesn't agree on somebody you're hanging around with, it makes you want to be around them more. I feel restricted, and like a little kid. Like they are controlling my life, like they think I'm stupid. I always feel like I guess I'm kind of claustrophobic or whatever when someone tells me I can't do something. I just want to prove them wrong."

DON'T PUSH THIS BUTTON

Reacting in the opposite way to commands is a natural reaction for teenagers. Without a solid explanation about "why not," many teenagers will bully their way forward, spurred by a combination of courage, obstinacy, and curiosity. This reaction is an understandable demonstration of human nature, especially among teenagers struggling to act independently.

Though this tendency is prevalent among teens, it is not unheard of among adults. Back in the days of mainframe computers with lots of buttons and lights, I worked as a programmer/analyst. One evening my teammates and I were working late on a project, trying to run a series of program tests. To make things difficult, there was a problem with the computer which repeated itself whenever the system was "powered down." If we just kept the computer running, all was well, but if we turned if off, it could take hours to repair and adjust and restart. The answer, which seemed simple enough, was to leave the computer running.

This solution required altering the department's normal procedure, which was to turn the computer off at the end of each eight-hour shift and restart it with a new configuration of tape drives and disk drives to fit the scheduled workload. To prevent the computer from being shut down, we wrote a large note with a bold marker pen and taped it next to the POWER OFF button. The note said, "Don't push this button."

When the late shift computer operator arrived for the evening, the first thing he did was walk up to the note and ask, "Why not push the button?"

"Don't touch it, Wally," we all replied. "The system won't restart if you turn it off."

Wally said, "It shouldn't do that."

Then we watched in disbelief as Wally pushed the button. Exhibiting all the emotional maturity of a thirteen-year-old, he was fulfilling his need to experience things for himself instead of accepting the advice of others—

not unlike the natural teenage urge to live life rather than just hear about it. Like every parent who observes as their teen specifically ignores an instruction, we were astounded by Wally's actions. Almost apoplectic with anger and frustration, I was also struck by the pure absurdity of the situation. How could Wally ignore such a specific warning? What was it about that sign that practically invited him to do the opposite of what was asked? It was almost as though the word "don't" had triggered a chemical reaction in his brain that caused him to rebel.

Parents recognize this contrary behavior in their teenagers, and agree that an overbearing, commanding approach to the topic of smoking will not be welcomed by teenagers—and it will not be likely to work. For example, a focus group of parents has been asked to evaluate the logos and tag lines designed to discourage kids from smoking. They have similar reactions to the tag lines that include the word "don't."

Suzanne has a part-time job but is always home to send the kids off to school with a good breakfast, and she's back home in time to make dinner for the family. Suzanne is active in the parent-teacher organization at her son's high school. She is a volunteer for fundraisers to buy uniforms for the school band, to add books to the library, and to send the cheerleaders to the state-wide competition in a newer, safer van. Suzanne is not afraid to speak up first. "This logo here with the words 'Don't Smoke Under 18'—that's the worst thing you could use. If you want to be sure they'll smoke, just tell them 'don't.' That will make them want to do it, even if they never thought of it before."

"If you just order them around, kids won't listen," says Bert, a contractor with a wife and two teenage girls. The girls are on their own after school most days. Though most of the parenting issues are left up to his wife, Bert sets the rules about certain things. His girls are not allowed to smoke or drink, and they have to show respect to their mother and to him. "Don't start a sentence with 'don't,' or they'll think it's just another command to ignore," Bert says, "They resent being told what to do. That's like preaching to them, and it's a negative. They'll do it just to spite you if you come off being bossy."

Marilyn sells real estate and is very successful in her profession. An expert at reading people, Marilyn knows just which features to point out in a home to appeal to a customer. She is a lot less confident talking with her teenage daughter about how to handle the pressures of alcohol, cigarettes, sex, and drugs. "I've been telling her these things for years. Don't drink, don't smoke, and don't have sex. You gotta be direct with them. But lately, I don't know what to say to Katie. If I say 'don't do something,' then that's exactly what she does. I can't tell what she's thinking. She just looks right through me, or she rolls her eyes when I'm talking to her. It makes me furious."

IS THIS A TRAP?

As parents of teenagers who are faced with temptations and dangers every day, we may feel as though we're caught in a no-win situation. How can we tell our kids not to do something without provoking an opposite reaction? We certainly wouldn't say to them, "*Do* take dangerous risks." So if we can't say, "*Don't* take dangerous risks," then what *can* we say?

The positive approach actually has a successful track record. For example, Nike urges its customers to "Just Do It" as encouragement to express individuality, achieve "personal bests," and, of course, to buy their tennis shoes and apparel. The Army rallies prospective recruits around the battle cry, "Be all you can be." These slogans are individual and self-interpretive. They mean something to everybody, and something separate to each person.

Of the alternatives offered to discourage kids from smoking, all the focus groups chose the line "Be Smoke Free" because it offers a positive invective *to be something*, instead of wagging a reproachful finger and inadvertently inviting rebellion by telling kids "*Don't.*"

The slogan "*Wake Up—Live Big—Be Smoke Free,*" a hallmark of a number of successful youth smoking prevention programs around the country, is another example of a positive expression intended to be personally interpreted by each teenager. "Live Big" is a call to action inviting kids to engage in positive activities instead of dangerous or destructive ones. The phrase encourages growth and development, exhilaration and adventure, self-expression and personal achievement: learning, dancing, skiing, painting, skateboarding, singing, building—whatever kids are driven to accomplish by their personal interests and goals.

The concept behind the "Live Big" slogan is applicable to parents as well. We are trying to give our children valuable gifts: our wisdom, our judgment, and our concern. The way in which we package these treasures will probably have a lot to do with whether they are well-accepted. If you present your ideas in positive form and invite your teenager to experience life with gusto tempered by good judgment, your advice has a chance of being followed. But if you emblazon the word DON'T in giant letters on the wrapping paper each time you deliver a package of ideas, your teenager will probably relegate the contents to the trash bin.

PLEASE DON'T THROW ME IN THAT BRIAR PATCH

With little kids, reverse psychology can be an effective technique. In the famous Uncle Remus stories so popular among children, the wily Brer Rabbit outwits the gullible Brer Fox by begging not to be thrown into the briar patch. Of course, the briar patch is precisely where Brer Rabbit really wants to go—and exactly where his foe tosses him. This trick of asking for the opposite of what you really want can work well with small children. When my son Ted was a toddler, I used to "steal" kisses from him by saying, *"Don't kiss me. Dooon't kiss me."* So Ted would practically chase me to give me a kiss and a hug.

But with teenagers, especially in the age of Generation Risk, the threats are too serious to risk using reverse psychology. We have to be literal and explicit in telling our teenagers what we really want them to do, what is allowed, and what is not acceptable. But we also owe them the courtesy of explaining why.

Dana

Dana is feeling good. Dana just turned sixteen and got his driver's license yesterday. He is driving his dad's car and is thinking about getting out of this interview to get back on the road. His dad gave him about 50 instructions about what to do and what not to do with the car: where to park, how fast to drive, remember to slow down if it starts to rain, be sure to clean the frost off the windshield, and so on. Dana is wearing a gray pullover sweater, jeans, and a Duke Blue Devils baseball cap.

"I completely agree with the expression, 'Respect your elders,' but I don't think it should only be that. I think they should respect you as well. I think they should not, in every single situation say, 'Well, I'm the adult.' What's their point? I can do whatever I want. At least my dad discusses it with me and gives me a good reason. You think, 'If there's not a good reason, why should I listen to it?' My dad always gives me good reasons not to do stuff, and we also have that trust thing going on, so I try to earn his trust."

Teenagers respond to positive choices and positive interaction much more readily than to negatives. A friend of mine still remembers disciplining his toddler by smacking him on the hand and barking out briskly, "Don't" whenever the little guy reached for some forbidden item on the coffee table. What happened was that the little boy still reached for things—he just learned to wrinkle his face, hunch his shoulders, duck his head, and brace himself for the blow he knew was coming.

There are alternatives to saying "don't" we can choose to use, if we think about the impact of our words. Psychologists warn against using "negative commands" that influence us to do what we are being told not to do. It's just as easy to say, "Remember to come home on time" as it is to say, "Don't come home late." But the connotations are markedly different. In the first case, you are encouraging positive behavior and implying that your teenager plans to obey your curfew rule. In the second, you are giving a negative command. You are implying that your teenager plans to break the rule and that you must remind him not to do it.

Sometimes it helps to seek out positives.

CATCH YOUR KIDS DOING SOMETHING RIGHT

When he was sixteen, our son Ted got a summer job working for a framing contractor. He earned some money, built up his muscles, developed a tan, and accumulated some major points with his parents. We both felt Ted was displaying responsibility.

My reaction was to express a profusion of pride, admiration, and glowing praise: "I'm so glad Ted has a job. It'll be good for his self-confidence and self-esteem, and might even encourage him to study harder in school. I'm so proud of him. I think it's wonderful that he found this job on his own, and that he's getting up early in the morning every day and working so hard."

My husband's reaction was also positive, but was expressed in slightly different words: "It's about time he got a job. All he usually does around here is sleep, eat, and watch television." When pushed, he added, "He's acting more mature, too."

Teenagers need positive reinforcement when they are doing the right things—and doing them well. For some of us, it's instinctively easy to express our appreciation to our kids. For others, it may be especially important to make the effort to recognize and mention positives, so our teenagers know that we notice.

One of the reasons why teenagers may not want to spend a lot of time communicating with their parents is that not enough of that time involves positive feedback.

Julie

Julie is wearing a black skirt and a new blue sweater set that she really loves. The color makes her blue eyes stand out. Julie is looking at the ceiling. As she begins to talk, she pushes her hair back with her hands and hooks it around her ears.

"Kids won't listen if you start a sentence with 'Don't!' I think just in general, all parents want is just what's best for their kids, so they're always pushing, 'Do this, do that, do this.' They want you to be able to accomplish everything. The thing that just bothers most people is that your parents are so busy telling you what you can improve on and where your faults are, they don't really praise you, or tell you what things you are good at and what things you have done right. I know when my parents get on me, most of the time I do deserve it, but it's just like they always are focusing on that. They won't say, 'Thank you' when you do something right; or they won't say, 'You just did a good job' or whatever and praise you. That might be what makes kids get mad, that parents always tell you what you need to do. Personally, I'd like to hear what my positives are rather than being nagged all the time."

When you tell your kids "don't" you may be risking a dangerous and opposite reaction. You need to be positive with your teenager instead of negative, to build trust and understanding, and to work with him or her to help find the right variety of things to "do."

Try taking a positive approach to dealing with limits with your teenager. Discuss why it's against the law in every state for kids to buy cigarettes. Talk about other age-limit laws. Ask your teenager her opinion. Why are there laws against these things? Listen to your teenager's point of view about the rules you have established for her behavior.

Explain *why* these rules are important to you. Then give your teenager credit for the level of maturity she has reached. Let your teeen make some personal decisions. Be firm about the critical areas that affect your teenager's safety, and give positive direction. Find a better approach than simply saying "don't."

11

THE FACTS ABOUT SMOKING AND ADDICTION

To have credibility with the sophisticated and experienced teenagers of Generation Risk, parents have to be prepared with facts. You not only have to understand why teenagers are attracted to risks. You also have to appreciate why teenagers want to continue these activities even after the novelty has worn off.

For Generation Risk, information has clout. When you talk about cigarettes, you can get through to your teenager with *the facts about smoking,* especially if you have something to say that's *new* to your teenager. As with any other serious conversation you have with your teenager, you need to have your facts straight.

NICOTINE AND ITS EFFECTS ON THE HUMAN BODY

The physical impact of smoking and nicotine's effect on the body are much easier to measure and explain than the interconnected social and psychological effects mentioned in the earlier part of the book.

The nicotine in tobacco leaf is an integral part of cigarettes. Nicotine produces mild pharmacological effects on the human body, similar to those of caffeine, because it is a stimulant. Smoking generates minor, temporary increases in heart rate and blood pressure.

When a smoker inhales a cigarette, about 90 percent of the nicotine in the smoke is absorbed in the lungs. From the lungs, substances travel quickly to the brain, within about 10 seconds. The resulting process of electrical impulse communication in the brain, chemical reactions, and substances attaching themselves to receptors on the cell bodies in the brain to block or enhance the release of neurotransmitters is very complex. But the overall result is an increased focus, concentration ability, or alertness.

Nicotine is the chemical component of cigarettes most often described as being *addictive*. The strong desire for cigarettes that typically develops in smokers who have not had a cigarette for some period of time is attributed to the pharmacological effects of nicotine. The National Institute on Drug Abuse, for example, describes withdrawal symptoms from nicotine usage such as "irritability, craving, cognitive and attentional deficits, sleep disturbances, and increased appetite."

So once smokers become accustomed to cigarettes, they may look forward to smoking to relieve these negative physical reactions.

DISEASE

The Surgeon General of the United States has concluded that smoking causes a number of diseases. Statistical studies of cigarette smoking and various diseases show that groups of smokers have a significantly increased incidence of those diseases compared to nonsmokers. Research studies indicate that the risks are strong and consistent, and suggest that smoking causes or contributes to lung cancer and other diseases.

People who choose to smoke are accepting significant health risks. *Teenagers know that cigarettes are dangerous*, but many of them smoke anyway, and most of them try cigarettes at least once. The statistical evidence is strong. That's it. There is no alternative explanation for the increased risk of disease in groups of smokers. Experimental evidence does not refute the conclusion that smoking causes disease. Given all this evidence, wouldn't you conclude that smoking is a cause of certain diseases? Of *course* you would. And so would your teenager, *but he doesn't care.*

Craig

Craig has just finished two burgers and a shake from Wendy's but he's ready to eat again. He is seventeen now, and has been growing a couple of inches taller every year for about the last three years. Craig lives in an apartment with his mother and two younger sisters. His dad left about eight years ago and lives in St. Louis. Craig sees him once or twice a year and talks to him on the phone occasionally, but that's about it.

"What do I know about smoking? It calms you down. It relaxes you. It destroys your health. Ha Ha. Smokers are not a certain group. They're just random people. Cigarettes are easier to get than most adults expect. Fake IDs are real easy to get. If you want to smoke, you just do it, and you don't worry about that stuff. You think it's not going to happen to you . . ."

WHAT'S NEW TO YOUR TEENAGER?

Your teenager has heard the health warnings before, but he doesn't relate to outcomes that are twenty or thirty years down the road. Research published in the Surgeon General's own report on *Preventing Tobacco Use Among Young People* has shown that "knowledge of the long-term health consequences of smoking has not been a strong predictor of adolescent onset."

These researchers know that "virtually all U.S. adolescents—smokers and non-smokers alike—are aware of the long-term health effects of smoking and . . . adolescents feel inherently invulnerable in their characteristically short-term view."

Telling your teenager that cigarettes cause lung cancer, emphysema, or heart disease is old news to him. He has seen the Surgeon General's warning on the pack.

Your teenager wants to know something *new*—something that *relates to him.*

Jared

Jared is a sophomore in high school and plays trombone in the school band. Some of his friends smoke, but he doesn't—yet. Jared has dark hair and intense brown eyes with long lashes. His face is smooth and tanned. The beginning stages of a beard are sprouting on his chin. He is wearing a blue-and-green striped soccer shirt, jeans, and white tennis shoes. Jared has a serious look on his face.

"We all know there's risks with smoking. That's just a common thing. Smoking is bad. We know that, you know? Don't tell us stuff that we know. Tell us stuff that's going to help us choose what's right and what's wrong."

Well, here's something your teenager may not have heard before. A recent study conducted by University of California researchers indicates that "there is something uniquely bad about starting [to smoke] young." The study measured permanent genetic changes in the lungs of smokers who began as children or teenagers. The study concludes that the later in life people begin to smoke, the less risk of disease. Smokers who began smoking as adults were much more likely to reverse the physical effects of smoking after quitting than smokers who began earlier.

Building on this idea of the particular differences in youth smoking versus adult smoking, health education centers teach a wide array of programs about health-related topics. One of the key themes of their programs is the development of the body through adolescence and puberty. They stress that growth changes in the body are generally complete by age 19 or 20. So the designation of the legal age for drinking alcohol at age 21 makes a good deal of sense, and legal age restrictions on smoking have solid health reasons behind them, too. You can use this information to explain the *reasons* for these age restrictions to your teenager.

ADDICTION

Teenagers don't understand "addiction." When you're only sixteen or seventeen years old, it's hard to believe that you will ever have a hard time quitting cigarettes. Teenagers don't believe *they* will become addicted to cigarettes. The teenagers of this generation expect to challenge and conquer risk, and the threat of addiction means little to them. To complicate things further, the word "addiction" is overused: Nicotine is addictive. Coffee is addictive. Chocolate is addictive. The Internet is addictive. Heroin is addictive. Sex is addictive. Running is addictive. We hear about drug addiction, alcohol addiction, addiction to caffeine, addiction to gambling, and addiction to work. Addiction is sometimes used to excuse behavior that would otherwise be considered socially unacceptable. Addiction is often used in a positive way, to indicate a strong fondness for an activity and a sense of loss if the activity is barred.

A study in Finland and Scotland recently compared the physiological responses of people who considered themselves "addicted to chocolate" to a control group who liked chocolate but didn't consider it to be essential. There were significant behavioral differences between the groups. The self-described "addicts" ate twice as much chocolate on average as the control group, were more likely to show bulimic tendencies or behavior, and were more depressed, but there was *no difference in their physiological response* to chocolate consumption.

This result implies that addiction to chocolate may have strong psychological dimensions that extend beyond the physical body responses to drive people to consume chocolate. This interaction between physical, psychological, and perhaps social factors is typical of many of the behaviors we describe today as "addictive."

Researchers acknowledge that there is considerable confusion regarding the nature of addiction. One definition of addiction is "a behavioral syndrome where procurement of a substance seems to dominate the individual's motivation and where continued intake seems necessary to maintain optimal psychological functioning of the individual." So-called withdrawal symptoms and physical dependence can be part of addiction, but don't really define it.

Another way of identifying addiction is that it "takes over your life, preventing a healthy balance of activities, goals, and relationships."

So what do all these definitions mean when it comes to talking to teenagers? Does addiction mean the insidious, corrupting entrapment of victims? Is it just another word for habitual behavior? Or is it something more complex? In fact, addiction is something so complicated that parents need to tread carefully in discussing it with their teenagers.

Here's the potential paradox for parents:

If parents blur the meaning of the word "addictive" through overuse, or *minimize or understate* the addictive nature of cigarettes, teenagers are likely to smoke without regard for future consequences. But exaggerating the addictive nature of cigarettes can be equally harmful because it can lead a teenager to think he is hopelessly "hooked." The most important determinant of whether people are able to quit smoking *is their belief that they can quit.* If teenagers are already smoking, and if parents over-empha-size the idea that they are "addicted," then these kids may be discouraged from even trying to quit.

Even worse, equating nicotine addiction to heroin or cocaine addiction implies that smoking cigarettes and using these drugs are somehow on an equal level. This argument trivializes the potential short-term horrors of illegal drug use. Parents should *never* imply that heroin is anything but incredibly dangerous. Heroin use has *drastic implications*: intoxicating effects that interfere with normal everyday life and mental functions, potentially life-threatening withdrawal symptoms, and the danger of fatal overdoses.

Quitting Is Difficult But Perfectly Possible

When any substance or behavior is taken away, a reverse reaction happens. If the substance was calming you down, then you are likely to become more tense when it is taken away. If the behavior was helping you feel comfortable in social situations, you will probably feel uncomfortable or awkward when you can no longer rely on it. *Of course* it's difficult to stop smoking. The more enjoyable the experience, the more difficult it will be to give it up.

Parents need to understand that *teenagers can quit smoking,* but that the process is likely to be difficult because it is driven by so many interre-lated factors, many of them more intense for teenagers than for anybody else. Smoking is a complex sensory and psychological experience that teenagers are unwilling to abandon without strong motivation. That's why building a solid foundation of facts and trust is a prerequisite starting point for parents and the teenagers of Generation Risk.

You can get help from many outside sources through structured quitting programs and support groups for your teenager. And you can provide encouragement at home. Most importantly, you can help your teenager decide not to smoke, because unless it's his decision, he just won't follow through.

You have an opportunity to show your teenager that you are aware of the pressures of life *today*. By understanding the facts about smoking, disease, and addiction, you establish a base of credibility with your teenager. He can believe that you know about things that affect him, and things that are different now than when you were a teenager. Your teenager doesn't have to rely on MTV, the Internet, and his peer group for information. He can talk to you. Use the facts to show that you understand what your teenager is facing with regard to smoking. Use the facts to give him reasons not to smoke that are relevant to him.

12

REFUSAL SKILLS—MORE THAN JUST "SAYING NO"

The fear of not fitting in is the risk that most terrifies the teenagers of Generation Risk. When faced with choices, they are as vulnerable to peer influence as they are resistant to common sense. To contend with the powerful forces of peer pressure, teenagers need more than hollow slogans to fortify their resolve. They need a vision of independence that includes peer group acceptance.

At a time when their friends are experimenting with new behaviors and breaking the rules imposed upon them since early childhood, these teenagers need special skills to steer clear of danger. They are seeking new identities to separate themselves from parental control, and they are naturally attracted to risks their parents wouldn't want them to take. They want to be independent, but not isolated, and their fragile egos make them especially vulnerable to the lure of taking risks with friends.

Researchers believe the transition to secondary school brings with it heightened peer group pressure. On one hand, kids are encouraged to develop a sense of autonomy and personal responsibility by managing their time and activities in a variety of classes with different teachers and classmates. On the other, the bonds they have typically developed in grade school are threatened as they are confronted with a constantly shifting array of peers, many of them strangers, along with looser adult supervision. The nature of the secondary school routine is depersonalized and complex, and drives young teenagers to seek peer group social support.

Their conflicting desires for independence and self-sufficiency versus security and support cause many teenagers to engage in dangerous risk-taking just to be accepted into a group. More than anything, they need to belong.

Marcia

Marcia, fifteen, is wearing a cream-colored matching sweater set and a khaki skirt with beige platform sandals. Her toenails are painted mauve to match her fingernails, and her hair is pulled back into a bun. She spent about twenty minutes putting on her makeup and picking an outfit for the evening. This ensemble is her third choice. She doesn't want to look stupid or out of fashion. She is meeting some of her friends to go to a party after her interview.

"I think everybody wants friends. You don't care if they're good or bad. You need someone to talk to, someone to tell what you feel—things you really don't want to tell your parents. When I choose my friends, I choose people by whether they click with me—people I like being around. It's just like, if we click, then—I belong. I have a lot of friends who smoke every day and do a lot of stuff that I really don't especially want to do, but if they're cool to me and treat me right, then that's okay. For me personally, a big thing is acceptance. I'll hang out with the people that accept me and care about me or whatever."

As a parent, you must understand the strength of your teenager's need for peer group acceptance. It is one of the driving factors that will govern her behavior as a teenager.

Author Cynthia Lightfoot argues that *risks are vehicles for building or maintaining relationships among teenagers.* She believes teenagers feel they are expected to take risks as "the natural code of teenagers"—which is why a substantial portion of their risk behavior occurs only in the presence of other teenagers.

RISK FACTORS, PROTECTIVE FACTORS, AND ROOT CAUSES

But there is plenty of reason to believe that parents can still strongly influence their teenagers, even in the face of peer group influence. There is a growing body of research on how to influence kids to stay away from alcohol, tobacco, and illegal drugs. The basis of much of this research, and the key to understanding how to communicate with teenagers about these important topics, is to address root causes.

According to Dr. Steven Sussman of the University of Southern California, author of *Project T.N.T. (Toward No Tobacco Use)*, social influences are "the major determinants of tobacco use in youth" and prevention efforts are "best served by addressing those social influences."

Researchers now understand "risk factors" (which make kids more susceptible to alcohol, tobacco, or drug use) and "protective factors" (which help kids avoid these dangerous behaviors), and they have developed a number of drug abuse prevention programs based on these theoretical underpinnings. Because the root causes of so many risk behaviors are related, these programs have demonstrated impressive long-term reductions not only in smoking, drinking, and marijuana use, but also in the use of hashish, heroin, PCP, inhalants, and cocaine.

Risk factors increase the likelihood of negative or undesirable outcomes. Protective factors are more complicated and are not simply the inverses of risk factors. Protective factors not only directly affect behavior, they also mitigate risk factors. In other words, while risk factors may still be present, protective factors make the risk factors less influential and make it easier for teenagers to handle them without engaging in problem behavior.

One of the main strategies of many successful programs is *teaching teenagers to preserve friendships* while rejecting dangerous risks because teenagers depend so much on their friends.

Zachary

Zachary is into natural food. He has a part-time job at a nutrition store and prides himself on his ability to explain most of the products on the shelves to customers. Zachary is a vegetarian and is also concerned about animal rights. He is wearing hemp sandals, khaki shorts, and a bright yellow 100 percent cotton T-shirt with a George Bernard Shaw quotation printed across the front in bold black lettering, "Animals are my friends . . . and I don't eat my friends . . .." Zach is fifteen, and has been an animal rights activist for three years.

"I think a lot of people smoke just to fit in and to be like their friends. Some people do it to stay in the popular crowd or something like that. Just to be classified as somebody and not just be an outcast and by yourself all the time. That's the way I look at it. You need your friends because you can't really talk to your parents, you know? Most of the time, your friends know more about you than your parents. It's easier to talk with your peers. Because, I don't know, it feels like they can understand you more. They're going through the things that you're going through at this point in your life. I don't know, your parents, they're grownups. They're not thinking on the same wavelength as you are."

Professor Gilbert Botvin, director of Cornell University's Institute for Prevention Research, has worked for over twenty-five years in the area of preventing youth smoking and other youth risk behaviors. His top-ranked Life Skills Training (LST) program incorporates the important premise that social relationships are crucial to teenagers.

Broadly speaking, life skills cover the range of social capabilities kids need to get along well in life, especially during times of dramatic change such as their teenage years. The LST program teaches decision-making skills, taking responsibility, peer-pressure resistance, assertiveness, stress management, and basic social skills.

Studies on alcohol-related attitudes reflect the susceptibility of young children to peer pressure, as well as concern by students about their "right to interfere" with the decisions of others in choosing to use alcohol or drugs. The ability to stand up to friends in a positive way is fundamental to dealing with peer pressure and extends beyond defensive behavior to proactive interaction by teenagers.

The teenagers of Generation Risk are surrounded by peers who are engaging in dangerous risks. If your teenager is armed with life skills, he will not only be better able to resist dangerous suggestions from friends, but he will also be more likely to lead them toward more positive activities.

HOW KIDS THINK

There are other important concepts embedded in the Life Skills Training program. Based on the way kids learn and develop, Dr. Botvin explains that teenagers are likely to challenge absolute rules from the past as a natural part of their development process. "There's a developmental shift in the way kids think. Younger kids think in a way that's very categorical: black or white, yes or no. Gradually, as they move into the adolescent years, they begin to see the world in a more relative perspective, to see exceptions to the rules they once accepted as absolute."

Their need to break with the past and establish independence is borne out when kids talk about their feelings. They instinctively feel a compulsion to break free of parental dominance as they recognize opportunities to experience more of life for themselves.

Kim

Kim is dressed in deep-red knits. When she walked in, she was wearing a deep-red ribbed v-neck sweater that is now draped over the chair beside her. Now she is wearing a sleeveless deep-red vest over a long dress that comes down to the tops of her hiking boots. Kim's hair is cut short over her ears and on top of her head, but is long in the back, all the way down to the middle of her back. She is wearing gold wire-rimmed glasses. She is squinting and frowning at her geography book. Kim is a sophomore.

"It's like you want a life of your own. Your parents know every single little detail about you, every word that comes out of your mouth. Can't I have some personality, some individuality? Leave me alone. Let me have a life.

I've always had to listen to my mom or my dad about everything. I want to go out and see stuff for myself, so that's why I might go against the rules. Parents seem to think that whatever they say, their child is going to actually listen. The bottom line is that you're going to find out for yourself. Always."

Understanding the power of the peer group makes it easier to understand why traditional approaches to keeping kids away from cigarettes, alcohol, or drugs have not been successful with Generation Risk. Programs (or parents) who just focused on the health concerns were missing relevance, and according to Dr. Botvin, that's why they failed:"Traditional approaches were not successful because they focused on teaching abstract health information about the dangers of smoking or the dangers of using drugs. Although kids are aware of those dangers, they're not particularly impressed."

It doesn't work to keep beating kids over the head with health facts and trying to scare them into not engaging in risk behaviors by focusing on the inherent dangers. To be effective you have to know how to reach kids about issues that are of serious concern to them.

If you talk to your teenager about social influences instead of health risks, you have a better chance of helping him avoid problem behaviors. For example, you might notice that one of your teenager's friends is a smoker. Instead of dwelling on the long-term health consequences of smoking or trying to break up the friendship, you should concentrate on building up his social resistance skills. You have to realize that, especially to teenagers, friendships are incredibly important, and long-term risks are not. Instead of being an antagonist and creating resistance in your teenager, work on building skills and increasing protective factors.

One of the biggest protective factors for teenagers is the strength of the family unit. Dr. Botvin explains that "one of the protective factors that can help to insulate kids from risks is called 'family bonding.' It's very important that kids feel connected in a positive way to their family, to their parents."

Building family bonds with the teenagers of Generation Risk is not easy. You are balancing on a high beam, and there's a danger of falling off in either direction. Maintaining equilibrium is critical.

One way to connect with your teenager is to work together on developing his refusal skills. The subtle but critical difference in using a refusal skill versus simply saying no is tied to the fundamental teenage need for peer acceptance. Refusal skills represent practical ways to divert pressure and avoid confrontations with peers. Again the balance is all-important: deflect the threat; retain the friendship.

Most of the effective prevention programs today include significant emphasis on peer pressure resistance skills. The "Preparing for the Drug Free Years" program developed by Dr. David Hawkins and Dr. Richard Catalano at the University of Washington, for example, describes three goals for Refusal Skills: "to keep your friends, to have fun, and to stay out of trouble."

These skills are based on a brand of common sense that seems so often to elude the teenagers of Generation Risk. Simple tips such as changing the subject to something more positive or repeating a refusal in the same words over and over can wear down even the most adamant invitations to danger.

Another technique is to make a contract with your teenager that she can fall back on under pressure from friends. If she can blame any refusal to take a dangerous risk on anticipated repercussions from parents, then friends will have a reason to accept her resistance to risk.

"GOOD CHOICES" AND "BAD CHOICES"

Father Matt Eyerman believes peer pressure resistance skills are much more powerful if they are based on concrete beliefs. An example of one session in the program he helped develop for teenagers at St. Agatha Church in the North Lawndale neighborhood of Chicago contrasts "good choices" with "bad choices" by using visual demonstrations. He piles such items as cigarette packs, bottles of liquor and beer, and R-rated movies on the "Bad Choices" table. On the "Good Choices" table is a glass of water. Father Matt uses these props to provoke discussion and thought. He explains:

"The kids react at first by saying, 'Aw, just a glass of water? That's not attractive. What's so great about that?' The answer is, 'Think about what's going to keep you alive. Then think about these other things, because they can hurt you.' When they can see and feel something, it makes a much stronger impression than words alone."

The St. Agatha program emphasizes letting kids work out their own solutions. Because fitting in is so important to the teenagers of Generation

Risk, they have to find ways of making good choices acceptable. Father Matt says that it's not enough to explain the dangers of risk activities to these kids:"Statistics don't work. Discussions work. Kids have to get feedback from each other to build their confidence, so it really helps to encourage kids to talk about these problems with each other."

You can help your teenager by practicing together hypothetical peer pressure conversations, and providing some techniques for deflecting pressure.

"How about a cigarette?"
" *I don't smoke.*"
"What's the matter, are you afraid your mommy will catch you?"
"*I don't smoke.*"
"Aw, come on. Don't you want to be part of our group?"
"*Sure, but I don't smoke.*"

Practicing peer pressure resistance skills with your teenager can give you important insights into your teen's beliefs. Many risks are misunderstood by teenagers who just listen to the surface layer of warnings about cigarettes, drugs, sex, or alcohol. They think that using a condom makes teenage sex okay. They have invented a new word that defines what they consider the only real danger associated with teenage alcohol use: "*drinkinganddriving.*" They mistakenly think that as long as they don't get behind the wheel of a vehicle, drinking poses no threats.

If you work together on developing responses to invitations to dangerous risks, you can personally build up your teenager's knowledge of the facts as well as his ability to use them. You can reinforce the concepts of successful prevention programs at home, help your teenager build skills, and help prepare him to make his own decisions.

Ryan

Ryan is wearing snakeskin cowboy boots. They are pale yellow with a sort of black underskin. The pointed toes are tipped with silver. His belt is made of matching yellow leather and has a large silver buckle with gold trim. He is wearing jeans and a blue denim shirt open two buttons down. Ryan is seventeen. Most of his friends like to dip snuff.

"You want to have your own decisions. You want to learn from them. You want to take charge of yourself and make your own decisions. I can learn from my own mistakes. If I go out there and do the wrong thing, I want to let that be the way to teach myself that I know not to do that again. It's training yourself. Then once I decide, I just need a way of letting my friends know that I'm still part of the group, even if I'm not doing everything they do."

Author Lynn Ponton asserts that we "betray our teenagers" when we assume that all risk is bad. She explains "a major attitude shift is needed" among parents regarding risk-taking. Teenagers grow by taking risks, so parental support is needed to encourage positive risks. At the same time, parents must identify and intervene to prevent *dangerous* risks.

Risk-taking is normal behavior. What is important is to distinguish between behaviors that are enhancing to adolescents versus those that are just dangerous. The attraction of risk is that outcomes are always uncertain. Only sometimes are the consequences negative.

According to Dr. Michael Resnick, who developed the Adolescent Health Study, "The main threats to adolescent health are the risk behaviors adolescents *choose*." By building their refusal skills, we enable our teenagers to defend their decisions when they choose to avoid dangerous risks.

13

WHAT IF YOU SMOKE?

Many adults are concerned about sending conflicting messages to kids about what's acceptable. Parents who drink liquor, for example, may be uncomfortable dictating to their teenagers that no drinking is allowed until age twenty-one. Parents who smoke may feel uneasy about setting rules for their teenagers about not smoking.

You may feel you are on weak ground trying to institute rules that you yourself do not follow. But if you are a smoker and you ask that your teenager *not smoke*, you are in fact abiding *by applicable rules*. Those rules are the laws in every state that stipulate minimum age limits and forbid the sale of tobacco to minors. What's legal for you is not legal for your teenager. There's nothing contradictory about that.

Our society has decided that kids should not smoke, just as we have established other norms to which everybody must conform. We have jointly judged that children should be protected from making decisions that could endanger them until they are mature enough to consider the consequences in a reasonable way. We have decided that alcohol and tobacco are not intended for minors.

Generally the behaviors that are considered "okay" for adults but not for kids relate either to physical or emotional maturity. There are minimum age laws for working, age laws for marriage, restrictions on admission to bars or R-rated movies, and restrictions on gambling. There are generally recognized minimum age ranges for leaving kids unattended or allowing them to stay out late at night or swim in the deep end of a public pool.

Overall, there are logical reasons for most of these rules, and as a parent you can rely on the support of society for your decisions to limit the freedom of your teenager. But you have to be especially careful with the teenagers of Generation Risk. They are educated about the adult world. They think they can handle adult behaviors, and they are confused about mixed messages from the world around them.

Jonathan

Jonathan is wearing a gold chain around his neck, a yellow golf shirt with a small polo player logo on the pocket, and khaki shorts. Jonathan is on the golf team and plans to go to the driving range after his interview, then to his girlfriend's house. Jonathan is seventeen, and is pretty busy most of the time. He doesn't spend much time at home, but his mom usually comes to his golf matches.

"How about a little consistency? I mean, there's so much pressure on us to have sex. Like there it is all the time on TV, but then there's ads on TV telling us not to. It's like they're telling us not to, but they're saying it's okay. Like you don't hear about abstinence as much as you hear 'safe sex.' What's that? You don't want me to have sex, but you give me a condom. Okay, that makes a lot of sense. And when we turn on Jerry Springer . . . that's like the national sex advertisement, right there. Have sex as much as possible, advice from Jerry Springer."

As a parent, you are being consistent, logical, and fair when you differentiate between what is acceptable for adults versus teenagers. You are backed up both by laws and social customs, and you have a right and an obligation to enforce rules about smoking and other risk behavior with your teenager. What's critical is that *your message to your teenager should be clear and consistent.*

Yet even with consistency, you know that teens like to take risks and that smoking cigarettes is a favorite one. You are right to be concerned that your child may be particularly tempted by cigarettes because you smoke and because cigarettes are available. There are some additional precautions you can take.

HOW TO HELP YOUR TEEN STAY SMOKE-FREE

The National Longitudinal Study on Adolescent Health has identified "easy household access to cigarettes" as one of the risk factors contributing to teenage smoking. So be sure you do not make your cigarettes easily available to your teenager.

Use your judgment to limit smoking around your teenager, and resist any impulse you might have to send your child on an errand to buy your cigarettes. Be conscious of your comments about your enjoyment of smoking. You don't want to build up the smoking experience in your teenager's mind.

Since nearly 25 percent of adults smoke, there is a certain level of social acceptability associated with smoking. Cigarettes are sold in over 320,000 retail stores across the country. Cigarette companies sold over 400 billion cigarettes last year. Teenagers know they have access to cigarettes.

If you are a smoker, there's no point in hiding your behavior. In fact, there are several ways to put your experience as a smoker to positive use.

IF YOU WANT TO QUIT

If you want to quit, you can be encouraged by the fact that nearly forty-five million Americans have stopped smoking. That's about half the people who have ever smoked. According to the Surgeon General, over 90 percent of those people quit without any outside help. So it's certainly possible to quit.

If you have tried to quit and failed, you can point out to your kids how difficult an experience that can be. If you are having trouble quitting, you can enlist the help of your teenager in building your resolve. You can also turn to any one of a number of organizations dedicated to helping you quit smoking. Tips on how to quit are easily accessible on the Internet. Try a few of these tips, such as the following from a Web site called "Nicotine Free Teens":

• If you've tried to quit before and failed, your chances of success are better . . . not worse. Most tobacco users who try to quit don't succeed the first time. With each attempt to quit, you learn something new. The combination of these learning attempts prepares you for the final drive to success.

• Don't smoke automatically. Make yourself aware of each cigarette by using the opposite hand or putting cigarettes in an unfamiliar location or a different pocket to break the automatic reach.

• Quit tobacco the way you started . . . gradually. You did not get to the point where you are overnight and it is unrealistic to think you can quit overnight. By quitting gradually you learn new coping skills each step of the way.

These are good suggestions. Quitting is not easy for many people, but it can be done. You can quit if you believe that you can quit. There are plenty of Web sites, health-care organizations, local hospitals, and smoking cessation programs available to help you if you want to stop smoking and are having trouble on your own. Consumer guidelines are available in printed form and on the Internet. As one example, the Agency for Health Care Policy and Research in Silver Spring, Maryland, offers free copies of the consumer guideline, "You Can Quit Smoking." They advise that "the more support you have, the greater your chance for success."

The basic advice of most of these systems is to keep trying (because multiple quitting attempts are often needed), to consider nicotine replacement therapy, to get support, to learn to handle the urge to smoke, and to reward yourself for success. (If you try nicotine replacement, follow instructions carefully and be sure not to double up on nicotine.)

Health organizations also provide tips for how to handle the first few days after quitting, centered around "thinking positive thoughts," "stressing constructive thinking," and "drinking large quantities of water and fruit juice [instead of] alcohol, coffee, and other beverages that you associate with smoking."

There are formal quitting programs available from the American Cancer Society and the American Lung Association, partnership programs with makers of nicotine gum and nicotine patches, and quitting programs that offer hypnosis.

IF YOU WANT TO KEEP SMOKING

On the other hand, if you want to continue to smoke, you can do that too, and still be a responsible parent. Discuss the topic with your teenager, and explain why. Give honest reasons. *Then explain why you don't want your teenager to smoke.*

The Surgeon General's report says that just because *you* smoke, it's not by any means a certainty that your kids will smoke—and that you can exert a positive influence by disapproving of your children's smoking, being involved in their free time, discussing health issues, and providing encouragement about their school involvement.

By discussing your own behavior factually with your teenager, you show that you respect him. By giving your teen the latitude to make adult choices *only when he becomes an adult,* you provide a framework that makes sense, and you behave consistently with the laws of the land. By making it clear that certain choices are not open to a teenager, you are on solid and respectable ground.

Adult hypocrisy irritates kids and makes them lose respect. Teenagers resent it when they perceive parents living by a different, less-rigid set of rules without a reasonable explanation. Worse, they lose their bearings. If they think they see inconsistencies, they react negatively. You can't be a hypocrite and get away with it in front of the teenagers of Generation Risk. If you smoke, you should talk openly to your teenager about why.

Keesha

Keesha is a teenage mother who is only fifteen. She has brought along her two-year-old son Rydel. Rydel is wearing jeans, a sweatshirt, and a tiny pair of tennis shoes. Keesha works at Burger King on weekday afternoons and weekends while her mother watches Rydel.

"My mom drinks but says, 'Don't do drugs.' I think that's hypocritical. She tells you not to do something, but she's doing something just as bad. I think, 'Why are you doing it?' It makes me feel like I can't respect her or something. Anything hypocritical gets on my nerves. Because my room will be messy and my mom's like, 'Clean your room.' Then I go out and look in her car. The inside of the car is real gross. I'm like, 'Why don't you go clean your car?' It's a double standard, and it makes me really mad."

Teenagers are constantly watching parents for signs of inconsistency. Generation Risk is testing, probing, and challenging the rules to test your mettle and your convictions. Your behavior is being scrutinized, and you are being judged by your teenager.

Not many people can stand up to such a regime of inspection if they feel they must behave flawlessly. As a parent, you have a job to do regardless of your shortcomings and foibles. You still have the incredibly important accountability of setting and enforcing boundaries for your teenager.

Brenda

Brenda is a vegetarian. She decided last year that she will no longer eat meat or eggs, and she has been cooking her own meals ever since. Brenda is wearing a yellow hemp shirt and denim skirt with braided sandals made from natural products. Brenda has long blonde hair and brown eyes. She is a junior in high school. Brenda's mother works as a loan officer in a bank, and her father sells building supplies. Neither of her parents gets home before about 6 P.M., so Brenda is on her own for several hours every day. She is usually out with her friends anyway.

"Well, your dad may be saying, 'Don't you dare drink. That's bad. That's the worst thing you can do.' And he's sitting there with a beer in his

hand telling you this. It's just kind of like, you've kind of got to explain why you're doing what you're doing if you want me to listen to you."

You can make things easier on yourself and your teenager if you open up your own behavior for discussion instead of making it off limits. Mutual respect is the best basis you can develop for strong communications with your teenager, and you must earn your share. Being open doesn't necessarily mean being equal. As long as you are willing to talk about why, it's appropriate to have different rules for yourself versus your teenager.

Michelle

Michelle has to work late tonight at Publix, checking groceries. She is already wearing her uniform because she won't have time to go home and change after her interview. Her boyfriend always teases her about how "cool" she looks in her uniform. Michelle is a junior in high school and plays on the girls' basketball team. She works on weekends to make extra money. Michelle looks tired.

"I don't really like it when my parents set up standards, but I understand it. It's not okay for me to drink, because I'm not over twenty-one. But it's okay for them. It's okay for my dad to tell me not to do things, because I live in his house, and he's my boss. It's okay for your parents to do things, because they're grown and they can. That's what you can look forward to when you're older. You can make your own decisions. In the meantime, it gets you kind of irked when your parents don't let you do things, but you have to look at it from their point of view, too. They want you to succeed."

If you take the time to communicate with your teenager about these important issues, you can help him understand that certain behavior is allowed for adults and not for teens. Teenagers are much more accepting of rules when the rationale is explained or when they see things in the context of childhood versus adulthood. *They just want you to explain why.*

Worse than being a hypocrite is being an ostrich. If you smoked pot when you were a teenager, get used to the idea that your kids are probably smoking pot today. It doesn't help to stick your head in the sand. In a national study by the Partnership for a Drug-Free America, researchers found that parents who are part of the Baby Boomer generation are not well-informed about marijuana usage among the current generation of teenagers. Only 21 percent of parents acknowledge the possibility that their teenager might have tried marijuana, but 44 percent of teenagers say they already have. Just 38 percent of parents think their teens might have been offered drugs, while 60 percent of teenagers report that they have.

These statistics do not mean that teenagers can't be reached by adults, or that parental interaction is too late. But the sad fact is that many parents fail to spend enough time with their teenagers. According to the National Longitudinal Study on Adolescent Health, since 1960 children in the U.S. on average have lost ten to twelve hours per week of parental time. That makes the time you spend with your teenager more important than ever.

If you expect your teenager to learn from your mistakes, think again. Teenagers don't just want to *know* things. They want to *learn* things. If you want to help your teenager, use your experience to relate to his feelings. Don't force him to relate to yours. Open up your behavior to discussion, and encourage your teenager to open up as well.

You can't live your teenager's life for him, but you can have a big influence on his choices. You shouldn't feel any less adamant about trying to protect your teenager from the risk of smoking just because you are a smoker.

14

CAUGHT IN THE ACT: WHAT TO DO

Nothing you do is going to keep your teenager from taking risks. In the age of Generation Risk, there is massive opportunity for risk-taking, and teenagers want to be included. All of the pressures of modern society are magnified by teenage insecurities, curiosities, and hormones. To cope with stress, to experiment, to have fun, to fit in, or simply because it's against the rules, all teenagers take risks.

Much of this risk-taking is healthy and developmental as teenagers confront challenges, confirm their understanding of themselves and each other, and test their capabilities. The teenagers of Generation Risk are especially prone to risk-taking because of their heritage, their environment, and the task they set themselves of outdoing their parents.

This generation of teenagers loves risk. They have grown up with it, and they seek it out. Heady with the power to make their own decisions, many of these teenagers mistakenly believe that they can handle risk.

But rarely do teenagers stay completely within the boundaries of common sense and cautious behavior. Instead they push the limits of safety and good judgment. They make mistakes.

As a parent, you should expect that even *your* teenager will make mistakes, and you should not overreact to minor transgressions. Otherwise your teenager will be sure you don't spot the major ones.

Jo Lynn

Jo Lynn is wearing black stretch pants, black clogs, and a gray turtleneck sweater. Her long dark hair is parted in the center and brushed back behind her ears, but it curls forward over her shoulders in large ringlets. She is wearing lavender eye makeup and clear lip gloss. Jo Lynn is fifteen and wants to be a television news reporter. She practices reading all her school reports in front of a mirror and thinks a lot about projecting her voice.

"Last year my parents found out about some little stuff that I really just totally regarded as no big deal at all. It was just normal teenage stuff, and they chose to act like it was a big deal and have a heart attack about it and tried to keep me in. So there's no way I'm going to let them know the more important things. I mean, I don't know if I'm going to smoke or whatever, but if I do I won't tell my parents."

You can count on not knowing what is going on in some parts of your teenager's life. Even teenagers who are very close to their parents need a certain degree of privacy and independence, and often these ingredients are mixed with risky behaviors. But there are often hints of problems when serious issues are at stake.

WARNING SIGNS

There are certain activities that should be especially alarming to parents. When teenage behavior is life threatening, parents must step in to break the cycle of ever-increasing risks before they spiral out of control.

The challenge for parents is formidable. You must allow your teenager to grow and develop and become independent, but you must also be prepared to provide appropriate direction, control, and discipline. The teenagers of Generation Risk do not yet have the appropriate judgment to accompany their boldness. They may feel they are being moderate in comparison to their peers, but peer group behavior is a flawed measuring stick.

Mark

Mark is sixteen, and is very conscious of the impression he makes. He dresses in loose-fitting, low-hanging clothes for free movement and to make a statement about his image. He is wearing a baseball cap with the bill turned to the back and sunglasses perched on the top of the cap to complete the look. He walks with a swagger.

"Yeah, I like to smoke, but it's no big deal. Some of my friends are into other things like doing drugs. You see other people doing things, and you get used to it. You think it's normal: sex, getting in trouble at school, getting a tattoo. I don't really take anything that I consider, in my mind, is a risk. Except I double the speed limit. Actually, I double the speed limit on a regular basis. But I can handle that. You know, if you see someone do a drug and they have fun or whatever, then it's not that risky. It might be risky to you your first time doing it, but after that, then it's not really a risk anymore, because you know you can do it."

For the teenagers of Generation Risk who do not see dangerous risk behavior as a problem, the role of parents is even more important. But the job of recognizing warning signs is not easy. Parents want to see their teenagers in a positive light, as in the old joke about the mother watching the parade: "Look at that! Everybody is out of step except my Johnny!"

This natural instinct of single-minded acceptance is a wonderful phenomenon in one sense because children need praise and encouragement, and they flourish with parental support and approval. But it's vital for parents to recognize those situations where teenagers are in danger.

If your teenager is smoking, maybe she is literally sending a "smoke signal"—sort of a coded message—that all is not right, and that some special attention is needed. One problem behavior can signal another.

The 1994 Surgeon General's report, entitled "Preventing Tobacco Use Among Young People," describes cigarettes as a "gateway drug" that could lead to the use of such substances as crack cocaine or heroin. What this warning really means to parents is not that smoking is going to lead to other problems, but that *smoking is a symptom of underlying issues* that could lead to other problems.

There are usually signs from teenagers when trouble is brewing. You should watch closely for warning indicators such as falling grades, poor attendance or misbehavior in school, dropping old friends in favor of new ones, changes (for the worse) in appearance, or apathetic or confrontational behavior. Many of these "signals" may simply be symptoms of the normal phases teenagers go through, and they may *not* mean that your child is smoking or drinking. But it is up to you as a parent to consider the possibility that even your teenager may be susceptible to social pressures.

Warning signals are not necessarily easy to identify. Symptoms such as "social withdrawal" and "feelings of being picked on and persecuted" are listed as early warning signs for school violence. But what teenager doesn't sometimes display these characteristics?

Warning signs for alcohol and drug abuse include "breakdowns in family relationships," "red eyes," and "persistent cough." Are they signs of drug or alcohol use, or are they indicators of teenage contrariness, staying up too late, and a winter cold? The American Academy of Child and Adolescent Psychiatry advises that "some of the warning signs [for teenage alcohol and drug abuse] can also be signs of other problems" and that "parents may recognize signs of trouble but should not be expected to make the diagnosis."

CAUGHT IN THE ACT

In contrast to some of these ambiguous symptoms of teenage programs, if you catch your teenager in the act of smoking, *you know* there is a problem. If your teenager is smoking, you must try to help him change his behavior because of the serious health implications. Even though teenagers may think they will be able to quit smoking any time, many won't quit.

You should also seek out *underlying problems*, because the consequences of other risk behaviors could be even more immediate and more devastating, endangering the lives of your teenager and others. Alcoholism, drug addiction, and drug-related violence are not bounded by social status, educational background, or heredity.

Many of the teenagers of Generation Risk believe that parents are out of touch with them and don't relate to the challenges of teenage life today. But more than ever, when signs of problem behavior become visible, it is vital to listen to your teenager to understand his perspective. It's urgent that you convince your teenager that you are accessible and can relate to his world.

Bart

Bart has red hair cut really short so the curliness doesn't show. He is wearing a beige sweater with a black horizontal stripe, khaki cargo pants, and chunky brown leather shoes. His sideburns are thick and long, and he is cultivating a small mustache. Bart is sixteen. His favorite band is Phish. He just bought their latest CD and wants to get back to his car to drive around and play it.

"My parents have tried to talk to me about drugs and stuff. It's like they're living in the past. It's like, what year are we are in? And the year they're in, it's like totally different. My mom always compares me to when she was my age and I try to explain to her that times have changed, but she still thinks that they are very similar. I'm like, 'No, times are way different.' Parents need to know that."

Our Own Son

There is no guarantee that you will spot warning signs if your teenager is engaging in problem behavior. Part of the challenge and thrill of risk-taking is getting away with it, and teenagers are skilled at masking their conduct.

When our son Ted was fifteen, I picked up his backpack one day to move it off the chair and *a pack of cigarettes fell onto the floor.* My husband and I were absolutely flabbergasted. Ted *knew* that we didn't want him to smoke. He seemed to be a well-adjusted, normal teenager with a nice set of friends. His grades were fine, his behavior hadn't visibly changed, and we didn't see the problem coming.

We struggled to keep our emotions in check. As the initial waves of anger and frustration surged, we wrestled against the impulse to berate Ted for deceiving us, for acting foolishly, and for disappointing us. *We didn't know what to do.*

We reacted as calmly, but firmly, as possible. We asked Ted to explain why he was smoking. He didn't think his behavior was really so serious—

just having a few cigarettes now and then with friends, just "to relax." We talked about the health risks of smoking, but of course Ted already knew all about those dangers—he just didn't think they would apply to him.

We recognized that long-term consequences were irrelevant to our teenager, so we applied some short-term consequences instead: no "going out" to socialize with friends, no talking on the phone, no ordering pizzas. Ted promised to stop smoking. He tried to talk us out of punishing him.

We implemented the penalties for a two-week period anyway, to be sure our son understood that this issue was a serious one, and we explained that if we caught him secretly smoking again, there would be a much more severe reaction. We made it clear that *this risk* was one that was out of bounds.

With driving age approaching, Ted seemed to be impressed. As far as we know, he hasn't smoked since. But we *don't really know*. It's up to Ted to govern his behavior when he's out with friends or home alone. Every teenager has the opportunity to smoke.

An Ongoing Concern

One positive experience doesn't guarantee success. As teenagers grow older, their privacy becomes increasingly important to them, and parents have to find new ways of staying involved with teenagers and monitoring their well-being. You can't systematically (or randomly) check their possessions and scrutinize their behavior without destroying an increasingly important bond of trust.

When children are young, they understand the need for close supervision, and they tolerate it. But when they get older, kids react differently to invasions of their privacy.

Brady

Brady is a senior in high school and is trying to decide where to go to college. He just assumes he will go to college. His parents expect it, and his sister has already graduated. But he doesn't have a career in mind. Brady is wearing a red plaid shirt with a beige lining around the collar. His brown corduroy Dockers are positioned low around his waist. His hiking boots add about two inches to his height.

"When I was a little kid, I felt different about my parents snooping around in my stuff. I mean, my mom used to check my sock drawer and I thought, 'Well, she's doing that to be sure I'm okay.' My parents would say 'When you live under our roof, you live under our rules.' It made sense. But now, I have to have my own privacy for my own stuff. If my parents went through my stuff, I would feel like, 'You don't trust me.' I'd find it really irritating."

Older kids want recognition that they are maturing. They feel that parents should respect them and have confidence in their judgment.

So what is the right balance? Parents have so many horrifying things to worry about:

- Will my child be safe in school?
- Are my teenagers downloading instructions from the Internet on how to build a pipe bomb?
- Are they mesmerized by hard-core pornography sites?
- Do they know how easy it is to get a gun?
- Are they using drugs?
- What can I do to keep them away from gangs?
- How can I help them stay away from cigarettes?

In light of all these issues, cigarettes might seem the least thing to worry about. But you have to be concerned about "the whole child"—everything that affects your teenager—and smoking is linked to low self-esteem and lack of self worth.

Cigarette smoking is not the least of the problems teenagers face. It's one of many problems, all of which matter tremendously. You can't separate these risks and deal with them one at a time. They are mixed together and blended like eggs in an omelet.

The teenagers of this generation are caught in a cyclone of risk-taking. They are storming through their teenage years searching for individual identities, battling for acceptance, and threatening to damage themselves. They believe they have reached maturity long before they have safely weathered the teenage experience.

If you catch your teenager smoking, *confronting the problem* is essential. Your reaction will make a strong impression and can either drive him away or draw him closer. Your teenager's self-esteem is on the line, but so is his sense of independence. He needs your respect as well as your concern.

Robert

Robert is tired of being picked on by his dad. It's nothing big—just little comments here and there that add up. Robert is 6'3" and could probably take his father in a fight. He's thought about it. Robert is wearing an Indianapolis Colts football jersey, jeans, and black tennis shoes. His head is shaved, and his neck blends into the back of his scalp like the bend in a thick rippled straw. Robert is sixteen.

"My dad judges you. Like I'll say, 'I did this today, Dad.' He'll be like, 'That was dumb,' or 'That wasn't a smart idea.' Or I'll be trying to tie up the trash bag and take it outside. Sometimes the trash bag won't come out and he'll say, 'You've got to be smarter than the bag.' He thinks it's real funny, but I don't like it. Anyway, I don't much care what he says because he's not really in charge of my life anymore. Whether they know it or not, our parents are done raising us."

Robert is right—and wrong. Your impact on your teenager can still be extremely strong, regardless of his expectations. But you can't decide for him. Your teenager must make his own choices about risk-taking.

What to Do as it is Happening

If you catch your teenager smoking, you have an opportunity to address a serious risk behavior directly. You have a chance to employ all the information you have amassed and the connections you have established to help him make a better choice.

Try applying these steps:

Calm down.

Your natural first reaction will be an emotional one. But displaying anger or disappointment will not be productive. Think of your discovery as a warning sign, and use the opportunity to discuss risk with your teenager in a productive and positive way.

Ask questions.

Find out what's really going on. Ask your teenager to explain how long she has been smoking, and how much. Understand her feelings about smoking. Assess whether she is a confirmed smoker or just experimenting. These factors will have a lot to do with your teen's ability to stop smoking.

Explain your concerns

Use factual information to convey your apprehension to your teenager. Put your feelings into logical statements backed up by your knowledge of what it's like to smoke and why it might be attractive to your teenager. Include health implications among your reasons, but don't limit your arguments to long-term consequences. Do more than just repeat old information. Show that you care about the underlying reasons why your child is smoking.

Relate the problem to your teenager, not to yourself.

Don't treat your teenager's smoking as *your* problem. Relate it to your teenager's well-being. Put it in the context of your teenager's life. Ask what smoking does for him, and why he thinks it might be difficult to give it up. Let him explain as much about his smoking as he can. Encourage him to reason through the pros and cons of smoking, and to come to his own conclusion to stop smoking.

Be firm.

Show your teenager that you are serious. Be consistent in your convictions against her smoking. Listen to her arguments, then offer your own. Be reasonable and patient, but be certain that you are right. Your teenager should not smoke. Don't let your teenager wear you down on this issue. It's too important.

Differentiate this risk from other teenage behavior.

Make it clear to your teenager that smoking is an unacceptable risk. Let him know that certain risks *are acceptable*, and talk about how risk-taking fits into the teenage experience. Discuss which kinds of risks make sense and which do not. Acknowledge that you can't police your teenager's behavior at all times, and let him know that you are depending on him to use good judgment.

Damn the behavior, not the teenager.

Remember that self-esteem is an important contributor to your teenager's ability to avoid smoking and other risk behaviors. Don't diminish his self-esteem just at a time when it may be low already.

Offer to help.

If your teenager needs help, offer to enroll him in a quitting program or connect with a counselor who can provide encouragement. Look up quitting programs on the Internet. Gather information from the library or local health organizations. Help your teenager find a support group and a system to help him quit.

Be patient, supportive, and available.

Remember that it might be difficult for your teenager to stop smoking, even if she wants to stop. She might fail on the first attempt, or the second—and have to try again. Give her credit for trying, and encourage her to try again until she succeeds.

The University Medical Center of Southern Nevada provides advice on how to help adolescent smokers quit, and suggests that there are three stages to the smoking cessation continuum: "I don't want to quit" (Stage 1), "I'm thinking of quitting" (Stage 2), and, finally, "Yes, I want to quit" (Stage 3). Depending on where your teenager stands, your strategy should vary. Going straight from Stage 1 to quitting doesn't work. Moving sequentially through the stages is a better approach.

The Agency for Health Care Policy and Research lists "being around other smokers," "drinking alcoholic beverages," "being under stress," "getting into an argument," and "feeling depressed" among the factors that "may cause you to want to smoke." Do any of these factors sound like descriptors for your teenager?

Appreciate that as a member of Generation Risk, it may be especially difficult for your teenager to quit smoking. Quitting programs are only effective for people who really want to quit.

If *you want* your teenager to quit, *that's not enough*. Your teenager has to want to quit, and the best you can do is to help him make that decision.

15

REACHING
GENERATION RISK

The adult world holds no secrets for the teenagers of Generation Risk. Their premature exposure to sex, drugs, smoking, and alcohol brings with it a level of stress not experienced by previous generations. It is more difficult to be a teenager today than when we were children.

The awkward social phase of adolescence is especially difficult for the young teenagers of Generation Risk who expect themselves to be able to handle too much too soon simply because it is within their reach. It's easy for these teenagers to be overwhelmed by the accelerated pace of their lives, and difficult for them to ask for help in a world that thrusts responsibility into their hands and exposes them early to a smorgasbord of risks.

As parents, we want guaranteed formulas to assure the safety of our teenagers. We want answers. We want foolproof techniques. We want *magic pills* to keep the teenagers of this new generation away from cigarettes, drugs, alcohol, and other dangerous risks. But there are no magic pills. What we must use instead is a mixture of common sense, determination, and deep understanding of the unique characteristics of this new generation and the threats they face.

DETERMINATION AND FOCUS

Reaching Generation Risk is an incredibly important and surprisingly difficult task. It's not enough to *want to* communicate with these adventurous, independent, and rebellious teenagers. To be successful in the context of all the competing forces that assault teenagers today, you have to use more than one approach as a parent, and you have to make more than one attempt. You have to block out the demands and stresses of your own busy life and be willing to *focus exclusively on your teenager*.

As a parent, you have a chance to influence your teenager's future more than anyone else does. This chapter explains twenty-seven ways to help prevent your teenager from smoking and taking other dangerous risks.

Think about each of these ideas individually, and use them together. Jointly, they will have a huge positive impact on your teenager.

1. Coach your kids through the critical teenage years.

Teach basic values and demonstrate techniques for making good decisions. Encourage your teenager to build personal skills in himself. Borrow techniques from athletic coaches or orchestra conductors: set goals and motivate your teenager to strive for them by repeatedly communicating the same message of confidence in his capabilities.

Build your teenager's self-confidence by gradually delegating more responsibility. Think of problems as minor setbacks that can be overcome through determination and practice.

2. RELATE to your teenager.

Talk about your teenager, not just yourself. Show an interest in your teenager's activities, feelings, and opportunities. Find out what your teenager is looking forward to doing. Ask questions that help you understand how your teenager thinks. Ask your teenager for opinions.

Remember that you belong to a different generation and that teenagers are keenly concerned about *their* issues, not just yours. Let your teenager choose the topic of some conversations. Resist the urge to dominate interactions. Spend time learning about something that interests your teenager. Listen to rap music. Watch MTV, sitcoms, and teen movies. Read the high school newspaper. Eat pizza together.

3. LISTEN completely and carefully to what your teenager has to say.

Resist the temptation to interrupt with answers. The bonding process requires that you give your teenager the chance to express complete thoughts and to know that you are really listening.

Maintain eye contact. Put away the bills, or the mail, or the ironing while you talk. Turn off the television and the computer. Focus on your teenager as if she has tremendously important things to say to you. She *does*.

4. Make your teenager a priority in your life.

Put your family in perspective, compared to all your other interests. Spend time and energy paying attention to your teenager.

Attend school or sports events that are important to your teenager, even if your teen doesn't specifically ask you to be there— but especially if he does. Follow through on your promises. Treat commitments to your teenager like important appointments that must not be broken.

Pay attention to your teenager. Notice his clothes and hairstyle. Remember when important events are coming up such as class presentations, tests, or project due dates. Help your teenager prepare for events that can either build or erode self-confidence.

5. Nurture trust.

Be honest and open. Believe in your teenager. Talk things through when trust breaks down, and start right away to repair the problems.

Assume the best about your teenager. Don't be put off by the shock value of current teenage norms such as style of dress, music, language, haircuts, or body art. Tell your teenager how important it is to you to be able to rely on his judgment and honesty.

Avoid hypocrisy if you want to maintain credibility. Explain your values, and do your best to live up to your own principles. Admit your weaknesses. Tell the truth.

6. Treat your teenager with respect.

Recognize your teenager for his progress toward becoming an adult. Give her credit for mature behavior. Expect her to accept responsibilities and to live up to bargains.

Acknowledge the incredible technical proficiency your teenager displays on the Internet, with video games, with the VCR, with the telephone answering machine—or with any of the dozens of other modern devices and skills that are second nature to the teenagers of Generation Risk.

Demonstrating that you respect your teenager goes beyond providing freedom. Another way to show confidence in your teen's judgment and maturity is to expect more. Depend on your teenager for something important.

7. *Allow yourself and your teenager to be human rather than "perfect."*

Be accepting. Remember that you were a teenager once, too, and that mistakes are a normal part of growing up. It's great to set high expectations and to strive for significant achievements, but leave room for a few errors.

The teenagers of Generation Risk need anchors to steady them in the raging storms of adolescence. Your ability to recover from mistakes can set a positive example for your teenager. If you take mistakes in stride, your teenager will be encouraged to learn from problem situations instead of being discouraged or losing a sense of self-worth.

8. *Be a good role model.*

Give your teenager a model to follow. Demonstrate the value of your advice by living a happy and well-adjusted life. Think of yourself as visible evidence that reckless risk-taking is not an essential ingredient for an interesting and fulfilling existence.

If you let the stresses of your life overwhelm you, if you become fixated on work to the exclusion of social interaction with friends and family, if you never take time to participate in enjoyable and relaxing activities—then your teenager will not be likely to listen to your advice about how to live.

9. *Enjoy your teenager.*

Spend time together doing things you both like to do. Watch your teenager do something that makes you feel proud. Notice something positive about how your teenager is developing, and give yourself credit for contributing.

Recognize the spillover effect of your emotions. If you are concentrating on positives, and if you are engaging in activities that are fun, then you will want to spend more time together. Conversation will become easier. You will confide in each other and become closer. You will build your teenager's self-esteem by showing that you appreciate her company.

10. Keep in touch with your teenager and his or her friends.

Learn the names and faces of your teenager's friends. Keep track of where they go and what they like to do. Learn some of the new words they use, even if their vernacular sounds like gibberish. Test yourself. Do you know what is most important to your teenager? Can you name his favorite musical group? Do you know how much time she spends on the Internet, or what interests her? Be sure you know your teenager as an individual.

You can't expect to be a part of your teenager's social circle, but you should know who is. Watch for warning signs of risk behavior in your teenager's friends. You can see them more objectively than you can see your own child. Appreciate how much his friends will influence him.

11. Acknowledge that teenage risk-taking is normal, widespread, and inevitable.

Understand that *your* kids are at risk, too. Remember that *all teenagers are vulnerable*, that all teenagers take risks, and that every parent needs to be involved to help teenagers assess which risks have unacceptable consequences.

Let your teenager know that you appreciate the aspects of popular culture that define current norms. Acknowledge that times are different today than when you were a teenager, and that decision making is tougher. Accept the idea that your teenager needs to take risks in order to grow and develop. Encourage your teenager to take risks, and offer to help evaluate "good risks" versus "bad risks" in terms of potential consequences.

12. Be lenient enough.

Listen to yourself. Do you always say "no" before you even think about the question your teenager is asking? Try granting a little more latitude. Try gradual steps, and give your teenager a chance to earn more of your trust.

The teenagers of Generation Risk are used to unprecedented levels of freedom in their day-to-day lives because they spend so much time with their peers and away from adult supervision. A home environment with unreasonably strict rules is ludicrous and laughable to these teenagers. Overregulation just challenges the adventure-seeking teenagers of Generation Risk to find ways of breaking the rules. You add to the attraction of dangerous activities if you outlaw them in absolute, unconditional terms.

You can't be there to police your teenager's actions every second of the day. You have to rely on your teenager's judgment and maturity. If you entrust your kids with the responsibility to make decisions, you automatically build their self-esteem by demonstrating your confidence and trust.

13. Be firm enough.

Exercise your right to set boundaries and your obligation to enforce them. Remind yourself that being involved is a sign to your teenager that you care. With hours of unsupervised time every day, the teenagers of Generation Risk have plenty of opportunity to drift into dangerous activities. They are more likely to get into trouble when they are hanging out with their friends than when they are in school or participating in organized after-school activities.

Make sure that the rules are clear and that consequences are understood. Identify which behaviors are unacceptable, and explain why to your teenager. Let your teenager see the intensity of your feelings about the activities which in your judgment must be avoided. Give your teenager a framework to lean on when making decisions.

Demonstrate that you are serious by following through when your teenager breaks the rules. Empty threats will erode your credibility. Make sure that the punishment is proportionate to the behavior. Differentiate between minor infringements and major rule breaking, and make sure your teenager knows you are serious about enforcing important rules.

14. Know the facts, and use them to discuss risks with your teenager.

Understand that smoking is a complex physical, psychological, and social experience. Resist the temptation to oversimplify smoking as merely an act of rebellion or a lack of willpower.

Address smoking in the context of friendships, insecurities, and short-term need fulfillment. Help your teenager reason through the pros and cons of smoking and conclude *on his own* that smoking is a bad idea.

If your teenager is a smoker, appreciate the difficulty he may experience in giving up cigarettes, and acknowledge the reasons why he may want to continue. Don't assume that threats of punishment or offers of incentives will be sufficient to motivate him to quit. Appreciate the strength of the attachment your teenager may have developed for smoking. Be patient as you work through the process of helping your teenager *decide to quit*.

15. Emphasize immediate consequences.

More than ever before, teenagers in the age of Generation Risk relate to immediacy. Their worlds are characterized by electronic-speed communications, networks, and computerized access to nearly everything.

Like generations before them, these teenagers feel invulnerable, especially regarding events in the distant future. But this latest generation of teenagers approaches risk with a new level of intensity and impulsiveness. They have been trained to be impatient and to expect immediate response. Understand that they will probably ignore even the most logical and compelling arguments about long-term consequences. Talk to your teenagers about short-term consequences they will care about.

16. Watch for "smoke signals," and get deeply involved when you spot them.

If your teenager's behavior noticeably changes, if your son or daughter drops old friends, or if moodiness sets in, find out why. Ask questions, spend time interacting, and be available. Make sure that you know what your teenager is feeling and what pressures are at work.

Remember that risk behavior may not be easy to spot because it is built into everyday activities for the teenagers of Generation Risk. But teenagers tell us that knowing parents are available to help them is critically important. Be ready to listen when your teenager wants to talk.

If you feel overwhelmed by the seriousness of your teenager's behavior, don't be afraid to ask for professional help. But don't expect to delegate involvement. Your teenager needs *your* involvement.

17. Find ways to say "DO" instead of "DON'T" all the time.

Remember that saying "don't" can be like issuing a dare, and can create negative or rebellious backlash reactions. Try to put things in a positive context. Loosen up on the little things to give emphasis to the importance of the big things.

Keep in mind that the teenagers of Generation Risk hate boredom. They have been weaned on multi-sensory, high-tech computer technology, and they are used to action.

Give your teenager the opportunity to be involved in life instead of being locked away from it. Demonstrate that your role as a parent is not to limit your teenager's fun, but to empower him and enrich his experience.

18. *Help your teenager understand his strengths.*

Catch your teenager doing something right, and praise him for it. Don't assume that your teenager recognizes his own personal strengths. Repeat and reinforce compliments. Give specific examples. Give positive feedback right away when the opportunity arises, before the moment passes.

Remember that nobody ever complains of having too much sincere positive feedback. The teenagers of Generation Risk have such a huge range of stimuli and overwhelming number of options that they often don't know what direction to pick. Help your teenager build on his capabilities to seize opportunities for success instead of focusing solely on overcoming weaknesses.

19. *Help your teenager develop social skills.*

Teach your teenager to sustain a conversation. Talk about what it means to be a friend, and how to develop new friendships. Help your teenager learn to ask questions, to listen, and to build on other people's ideas.

Appreciate the importance of your teenager's peer group and his need to fit in with his friends. Arm him with the ability to interact socially without depending on illegal substances for support. Build self-confidence by making him feel interesting, and show him how to carry on a dialogue with peers.

20. *Develop peer pressure resistance skills in your teenager.*

Practice techniques for saying "no" to bad ideas without destroying friendships. Give your teenager some safe experience to build his resolve and comfort level before he faces tough pressures alone.

Encourage your teenager to steer friends in positive directions when they drift toward dangerous risks. Explain that he doesn't have to be confrontational—that he can use humor to deflect suggestions, or that he can change the subject to something more positive. Teach him how to use the broken-record approach and repeat over and over, "No, I just don't want to do that."

None of these ideas will cause him to lose friendships. Teach him to resist peer influence and still fit in with the group.

21. *Allow your teenager to "save face" by deflecting head-on conflict.*

If you must criticize something about your teenager, aim at the *behavior*, not the person. Let your teenager be part of the solution, to help you deal with your feelings of disappointment, anger, or concern.

Work together to come up with constructive ways to avoid similar problems in the future. Your teenager *can't change who she is.* Your teenager *can change how she behaves.*

Confronting the teenagers of Generation Risk will increase their feelings of frustration and drive them toward rebellious behaviors. Remember that this generation of teenagers has an extraordinary range of options for high-risk activities.

22. *Give your teenager a chance to be angry sometimes.*

Allow your teenager to relieve the stress brought on by the unparalleled pressures she faces. Respect the intensity of frustrations and the depths of confusion that temptation-fraught teenage years create in the age of Generation Risk.

When your teenager overtly expresses anger, let the steam cool down. It will eventually condense. Exercise patience. Demand respect, but allow your teenager to work through feelings of anger openly. Popular culture creates unrealistic promises of glamorous and fun-filled teenage years and puts pressure on teenagers to engage in high-risk, high-speed activities. Acknowledge your teenager's right to be angry when expectations fail to match reality.

23. *Let go of old issues.*

Give your kids a chance to start fresh after they encounter problems. Prove to them that you will give them full credit for good things that happen in the future instead of repeatedly weighing their actions against old mistakes over and over again.

Use mistakes as mutual learning experiences for you and your teenager so that the same problems will not be repeated. But leave archeology to the professionals. There's no need to dig up old issues. Your teenager will feel frustrated and discouraged if you keep referring to incidents in the past.

Give your teenager a chance to build your trust. Evaluate each situation on its own merits, and do not let negative experiences in the past cast a shadow of doubt or mistrust over your relationship.

24. *Base your relationship with your teenager on more than power and authority.*

You are the boss, because you are the parent. But remember that power is easily abused and is much more effective when balanced with trust and empathy. Nurture your common interests and spend time together appreciating the qualities and skills your teenager displays.

Use humor, sports analogies, or animal stories to find common ground. Talk about popular culture. Take your teenager out to eat, one-on-one. Take time out from your other priorities. Talk about what your teenager wants to talk about. Make yourself available when your teenager is in the mood to communicate. Assume that your teenager has something worthwhile to say.

Learn the difference between listening and just waiting to talk.

25. Compliment your teenager on accomplishments and positive behavior.

Find opportunities to praise your teenager. Recognize progress toward goals, consistency in following the rules, and positive initiatives. Reinforce behaviors you'd like to see repeated.

The teenagers of Generation Risk thrive on pace and energy. They are like multi-tasking computers—they can watch television, carry on a cell phone conversation, and finish their homework assignments simultaneously. Take time to marvel at their capabilities.

26. Be supportive.

Encourage your teenager to participate in sports, clubs, or social activities. Let your teenager know that it's okay to fail sometimes and that taking a positive risk is a good thing because it can help her develop new skills.

Acknowledge that your teenager has a right to be an individual. Explain why when you don't agree with your teenager's choices, but don't force compliance on every minor issue. Support intelligent risk-taking that develops your teenager by building new capabilities without endangering him.

27. Use your dog to help you practice quality interaction with your teenager.

Think of your dog as a surrogate teenager. Scratch your dog's ears. Praise your dog and enjoy watching the warm and joyous response. Notice how your dog reacts to your moods, and how your emotions are transferred to your dog. Reflect on the awesome power you have to influence your dog's behavior, sense of security, and level of happiness.

Remember that your teenager needs even more attention, more love, and more positive strokes than your pet. Be sure that you begin each interaction with your teenager on level ground, and that you don't unload negative emotions on your already overloaded teen.

CONCLUSION

YOU ARE PIVOTAL to your teenager's life.

As your Generation Risk teenager wrestles with the contradictions and confusion of the modern age, you have a special opportunity to help your child safely through the difficult teenage years. You have the capability to influence your teenager's future more than any other factor in his or her life.

As a parent, you can build a connection to your teenager that is stronger than the combined power of peer groups, popular culture, and the World Wide Web.

As the parent of a teenager in America today, you have a distinct advantage over previous generations: *you understand risk*. You have open access to the exhilaration, adventure, and excitement of whitewater rafting, casino gambling, and on-line stock trading. Your generation pioneered the influence of teenagers as a force in American politics and social policy. You set the standard your teenager is trying to surpass.

Yet you are a parent, and you fear for your child's safety and well-being. You yearn to substitute concern, caution, and control for the risk in your teenager's life. You are instinctively tempted to restrict and limit your teenager, without realizing that too much control will drive your child toward rebellion and risk.

Fortunately, you have an opportunity instead to encourage positive risk-taking that strengthens your teenager's self-image and helps develop new skills. You have a chance to teach your teenager to give weight to the consequences of dangerous risks.

You have the tools to relate to Generation Risk and to keep in touch with your teenager regardless of the mutual pace in your lives. The teenage need to belong to a group applies to families as well as to peers.

217

Armed with the information in this book, along with loving concern, you have the opportunity to establish a better relationship with your teen—and, in the process, to help your teen recognize and bypass risks that are also invitations to danger. Your insights and guidance can provide a beacon of light through an otherwise dark and perilous tunnel. Use your understanding of this new generation—its strengths and its vulnerabilities—to build confidence and self-esteem in your teenager and to empower your child to choose not to smoke.

INDEX